Scarlett
rules

Scarlett
rules

*When Life Gives You Green Velvet Curtains,
Make a Green Velvet Dress*

Lisa Bertagnoli

VILLARD / NEW YORK

For my mother

If you wish to be loved, show more of your faults than your virtues.

—EDWARD BULWER-LYTTON

CONTENTS

INTRODUCTION

I first heard mention of *Gone with the Wind* when I was sixteen years old. My sister and I were in South Carolina visiting my father, and on a drive through a hazy, humid countryside thick with live oak trees, he suddenly stopped the car.

"Look," he said, pointing to an elegant white house set back from the road, half obscured by a curtain of Spanish moss. "That's the model for Tara."

"Huh?" we asked, straining to look from the backseat.

"Tara!" Dad said, bothered that we didn't immediately get the reference. "The house in *Gone with the Wind.*"

We didn't exactly believe him—my father was a pro at making things up—but somehow I'd gotten to be a teenager without ever hearing about *Gone with the Wind.* That house certainly piqued my interest. What kind of story took place in such a mansion, so different from our six-room apartment in Chicago? What sort of people lived there? What lives did they live?

When we returned to school that fall, I checked *Gone with the Wind* out of the school library, planning to read it between bouts of homework. I took a peek at the first page and started to read. Three days and no homework later, I finally finished the thousand-plus pages.

The belle of Tara had my heart from the start. Lots of girls have crushes of sorts on their friends, and I certainly had a crush on Scarlett. There was so much to admire. Her raven hair, emerald-green eyes, vast wardrobe of flowered hoop-skirted dresses, and, of course, that seventeen-inch waist. How did she get it that way? I wondered as I pulled a tape measure tighter around my waist. That was before I learned that corsets and whalebone stays crushed Scarlett's waist to a fashionable, yet unnatural, seventeen inches.

I could identify with some of my favorite fictional characters: awkward Francie Nolan in *A Tree Grows in Brooklyn*; Laura's Midwestern sensibilities in *Little House in the Big Woods*. Scarlett and I had nothing in common except dark hair. She was a saucy, confident Southern belle; I was a gawky, shy Northern girl. I adored the first line of the book introducing Scarlett as a girl so charming that men actually forgot that she wasn't beautiful. The idea that charm could trump beauty was a heady one, especially for a girl who felt she could run naked through a crowded high school cafeteria without catching the eye of a single boy.

Scarlett's story, though, was what kept me turning those pages. I met her when she was a sixteen-year-old girl most worried about what dress she'd wear to a barbecue. When I left her she was a twenty-eight-year-old woman who had survived the bloodiest war fought on American soil, been married three times and widowed twice, borne three children and buried one, suffered a miscarriage, killed a man, lost her mother to typhoid fever and her father to a terrible accident, and, despite it all, managed to make a fortune and hold on to her sanity.

Scarlett and her story drew me to the book not just once but twenty-two times—and twice more to research *Scarlett Rules.* I never did return that copy to the school library. It's still on my bookshelf, there for whenever I hanker for an absorbing, well-written book, lush with color and details.

Each time, I can't put it down until I finish it.

And each time, I learn something new about Scarlett.

Here's what I've learned so far: Scarlett is street-smart, resourceful, and down-to-earth. She's impulsive. Instead of whining about what she doesn't have, she works with what she's got. She changes with the times. She refuses to admit defeat.

But I find Scarlett fascinating because she's imperfect. Scarlett is stubborn. She's charming on the outside and a self-serving go-getter on the inside. She says the wrong thing at the wrong time. She makes friends with all the wrong people. She mistakes lust for love and confuses loyalty with weakness.

Over the years, I've come to regard Scarlett as a muse because of that very imperfection. I've learned as much from her weaknesses as from her strengths. Finding myself seduced by the idea of a person, just as Scarlett was seduced by her romantic visions of Ashley, I'll remember Scarlett and how miserable her illusions made her. Finding myself afraid to act, I'll remember seventeen-year-old Scarlett delivering Melanie's baby with the Civil War raging just outside her front door.

As much as I enjoy the movie, a beautifully made film that captures many facets of Scarlett and her story, I draw endless inspiration from my dog-eared copy of the book. It explores the essence of Scarlett's personality; readers, more than viewers, understand what makes Scarlett tick. The novel also portrays some intriguing relationships, among them Scarlett's friendship with Will Benteen, the soldier who arrived wounded on Tara's doorstep and rebuilt the plantation into a prosperous farm; Scarlett's relationship with Archie, the one-eyed ex-convict she hired to drive her around Atlanta; and Rhett's connection to Belle Watling, the brothel owner who may or may not have been the mother of Rhett's son.

And I must admit that, as much as I enjoy the story, certain aspects of it bother me deeply. Even casual readers of *Gone with the Wind* might wonder why I have chosen to present a slave owner as a role model. While Scarlett O'Hara is a fascinating, multifaceted woman—there aren't many female characters like her in literature—author Margaret Mitchell took a curiously cavalier attitude toward slavery. Mitchell used the n-word casually and wrote the slaves' dialogue in condescending dialect; she chose not to use dialect to give her white characters Southern accents. Mitchell described Gerald's purchase of Dilcey, his slave Pork's wife, as a magnanimous and gentlemanly action; she portrays Tara's slaves as happy and well cared for. Still, readers often make allowances for works of literature that are products of their times: The anti-Semitism in Shakespeare's *The Merchant of Venice* and the casual use of the n-word in Mark Twain's *Huckleberry Finn* come to mind. I ask readers of *Scarlett Rules* to make allowances for *Gone with the Wind* as the product of a Southern-born-and-bred author and her time and place, the Jim Crow South.

Women around the world know Scarlett. But they don't know Scarlett like I know Scarlett. And I want to share the wealth. So, based on my careful readings of *Gone with the Wind*, I've created twenty-four Scarlett Rules that can help women handle any area of life—romance, work, friendships, family—a little more effectively.

I'm hardly the only woman who seems to have taken a page or two out of Scarlett's book. Marry for strategy as Scarlett did, not once but three times? Consider Pamela Harriman, who, by virtue of her three marriages—to Winston Churchill's son, a Broadway producer, and a railroad magnate—vaulted from being a country nobody to becoming the U.S. ambassador to France and a Democratic Party powerhouse. Clearly, there's Scarlett in her blood.

Scarlett must run in Hillary Rodham Clinton's veins, too. Would Scarlett have been content to hold White House soirees and bake cookies? Not the Scarlett I know. Like Senator Clinton, Scarlett would have made herself a valuable—and visible—adviser to her powerful husband and then gone on to forge her own political career.

Just as Scarlett peddled her lumber through the streets of postwar Atlanta, Josephine Esther Mentzer pounded the pavement of post–World War II New York, pushing her hand-made skin creams until Saks Fifth Avenue agreed to give her counter space. Mentzer became better known as Estée Lauder, and the company that bears her name is now worth billions.

I'm not sure if Madonna's ever read *Gone with the Wind*, but the singer certainly has an aura of Scarlett about her. Just as Scarlett broke new ground when she became Atlanta's first businesswoman, Madonna broke new ground for female pop stars when she took control of her own career and launched her own record label. (Just as Scarlett married for strategic purposes, Madonna made boyfriends of many high-placed musicians early in her career, the better to learn from them.) Madonna, like Scarlett, became her own boss and now reaps the benefits: She's a millionaire many times over, a pop icon with millions of fans, and, best of all, she still calls the shots.

Scarlett O'Hara would be 161 years old as this book goes to press, in the year that marks the seventieth anniversary of the publication of *Gone with the Wind*. Big numbers, both, but to Scarlett fans, they don't mean a thing. Scarlett remains fresh, her life and experiences still meaningful.

There's no shortage of women in today's media-saturated world who have captured our collective attention, and fictional and real characters from Carrie Bradshaw to Paris Hilton keep us entertained and amused. Yet true role models are scarce; for that we need more than entertainment and amusement.

My dear, we need Scarlett.*

---

* You thought I'd say "*Frankly,* my dear," right? Wrong! *Frankly* was added for the movie.

Scarlett
rules

Scarlett
rule 1

PRETTY IS AS PRETTY DOES

Scarlett O'Hara was not beautiful, but men seldom realized it when caught by her charm. —Gone with the Wind

Beauty is all very well at first sight; but who ever looks at it when it has been in the house for three days? —George Bernard Shaw

Fans who've seen the movie yet not read the book all agree: Katie Scarlett O'Hara was beautiful. Drop-dead gorgeous Vivien Leigh brought Scarlett to life on the silver screen, and Leigh was perfect for the role. Her model-slim figure, wavy jet-black hair, and green eyes eerily matched Margaret Mitchell's description of our heroine—except for one important detail. Where Vivien Leigh's classic features made people stop and stare—"What a lovely child," commented Queen

Mary of England when the sixteen-year-old Vivien was pre-sented at court—Scarlett wasn't beautiful, a fact made clear in the very first sentence of the novel.

What made Scarlett different from every other average-looking girl in the world is that Scarlett was unaware of her lack of beauty. And if someone had had the nerve to mention that fact to her, she probably wouldn't have cared. Scarlett knew how to dress to play up her figure, and she knew how to act to make men (and women) forget she was anything but ravishing.

Scarlett's favorite gowns were green, the better to high-light her bewitching, catlike eyes. She wore hats and gloves to protect her milky-white complexion, so prized by Southern belles, from the harsh Georgia sun. When she could, she wore gowns that showed off as much of that peaches-and-cream skin as she could.

Scarlett knew that clothes make the girl. More important, she understood that charm almost always seals the deal. She knew instinctively that the perfect accessories for her just-right gowns were the Scarlettisms that *Gone with the Wind* fans know so well: fluttering eyelashes, a flirtatious smile, that calculated toss of her head. When she had harsh words to say, Scarlett sugarcoated her speech, smiling and fluttering those eyelashes all the while. Better than most anybody, Scarlett knew that it's not what you say, it's how you say it.

But Scarlett's charm was as filigreed as the French lace trimming her pantalets. Unlike Melanie, who was born gra-cious, or Ashley's sisters, who'd rather die than display any-thing less than impeccable manners and perfect charm, Scarlett's veneer carried her only so far. When Scarlett did not get her way, her Irish temper flared, her brow furrowed, and she forgot every single deportment lesson drummed into proper Southern girls.

Only when the upset world was righted once again and tilting decidedly in Scarlett's favor was she sweetness, grace, and charm personified.

On the surface, Scarlett had charm in spades. But she lacked true charm: the ability to be unfailingly unflappable, polite, and well-mannered even under awful circumstances. Had Scarlett been truly charming, she would have accepted Ashley's marriage to Melanie graciously and would never have let Rhett get under her skin, as he did so many times.

Truly charming people make anyone feel that he or she is the only person in the world. They know how to deliver a compliment and how to accept one. They know how to make people feel good about themselves and about life, no matter what the circumstances.

Like a mean backhand or a perfect risotto, charm is a skill that takes cultivating. What does it take to be like her, the woman whose entrance makes a party, whose smile is like the sun breaking through clouds, who's invited everywhere and then some? The next time you're at a party and spot a woman surrounded by people hanging on her every word, watch her. Take mental note of what she says and does in the company of her admirers.

This is what you'll learn: She listens. She doesn't interrupt. She doesn't reply to an anecdote with a quick "Oh, that happened to me once!" She lets the story, however trite, long, or boring, belong to the teller. She remembers people's names and details about their lives: new job, new baby, new home. If she doesn't remember a name, she graciously asks for it, because candidly admitting a lapse in memory can be charming in itself. She asks to see baby pictures, sparing proud new parents the awkwardness of an unwanted show-and-tell.

She gives well-considered, straightforward compliments with no hidden meaning. She'll say, "That dress looks great on you," not "That dress makes you look so thin." She'll tell you how gracious your home is, not that white paint makes the living room look so much bigger. You get the idea. A real compliment, one that makes the hearer blush with pride, carries not even the smallest piece of negative baggage.

A charming woman knows how to accept a compliment, even the backhanded type that she never delivers. She knows the proper response is a handful of words: "Oh, thank you. How kind of you." And that's it. No embellishment or argument needed. Not "Oh, this old thing?" Not "You've got to be kidding." A short, gracious response does the trick.

A charming woman lets people help her. When a man offers to carry her groceries to her car, she says yes. When a man holds the door for her, she says thank you. She doesn't even consider shaming him with a rant on how she's strong enough to open the door herself, thank you very much. It makes people feel good to help other people; a charming woman knows that.

A charming woman says *thank you* and *please*. She handwrites thank-you notes, even if she's already thanked the giver in person. She knows that anachronisms such as thank-you notes and letters are oh-so-welcome in this world of dashed-off electronic communiqués and mailboxes full of catalogs.

A charming woman knows that weddings and parties are a social contract of sorts. Attendees are expected to contribute to the atmosphere, not merely sit in a corner and observe. She responds to invitations promptly; when she says yes she shows up; when she arrives, she draws wallflowers out of their corners. She asks them about books they like, movies they've seen, vacation spots they adore. She doesn't ask about their jobs; that's a dead end and a possibly embarrassing question.

She also knows that wakes and funerals are necessary. She knows to say "I'm so sorry for your loss" to the mourners and leave it at that: no philosophizing or prognosticating on the deceased's current residence with God, angels, or other heavenly creatures. And when the bereaved appears at a social gathering weeks or months later, she knows to greet that person with a warm "It's good to see you again," not the tossed-off thoughtless "How are you?"

Why bother cultivating charm when life is filled with so many other demands? Here's one reason: It's the right thing to do. Think how much more pleasant the world would be if more people made even half an effort to be charming. And here's another: You never know whom you're going to charm. That person could lead you to a great job, a new friend, maybe even a spouse. Scarlett, our faulty heroine, was certainly at her most charming when she had something—tax money for Tara, a husband—to gain.

But here's the biggest reason to be charming: Beauty fades; charm lasts. As George Bernard Shaw observed, nobody notices beauty after it's been in the house for three days. Charm is noticed—and cherished—forever.

PUT YOUR BEST FOOT FORWARD

Not every woman has Scarlett's mesmerizing eyes or her tiny waist. But every woman does have physical qualities that, given just a bit of attention, can make her a knockout. According to Jesse Garza, co-founder of Visual Therapy, an image-consulting firm with offices in New York and Los Angeles, here are the beauty spots women tend to overlook.

Your health. Before he even takes a peek at their wardrobes, Garza counsels his clients to exercise and eat nutrition-packed foods. The result? Healthy, glowing skin and a body confidence that no Chanel suit can beat. "Nutrition and exercise give you the best version of yourself," Garza says.

Your hair. Shiny, healthy hair cut in a flattering style will elicit *wow*s wherever you go. Even if you don't spend a lot of money on your clothes, invest in a good haircut.

Your skin. Garza is adamant on this one: "Moisturize! Use sun block!"

Your clavicle. "That area from shoulder to shoulder is really beautiful," Garza says. Give it some attention with an elegant bateau-cut top; for extra pizzazz at night, rub in a bit of shimmery body lotion.

Your calves. Wear skirts tailored to a length that shows the taper of your calf toward your knee. "The curve of a calf can be super-great, super-sexy," Garza says.

Your back. Forget a plunging neckline; try a plunging backline instead. A deep V-back, a sexy drape, or a cowl gives people something to talk about when you leave a room.

Your overall shape. Every body has a shape, and women make a big mistake when they smother themselves in baggy garments. "It's better to create a waist and go with clothes that are more tailored," Garza suggests.

Your curves. Ankles, wrists, hips, shoulders, butt: Curves make a woman's body. Play up your curves with garments that skim them but don't turn them into sausage casings. "Curves are sexy done the right way," Garza says.

Scarlett
rule 2

DRESS THE PART

The rose organdie with long pink sash was becoming, but she had worn it last summer when Melanie visited Twelve Oaks and she'd be sure to remember it.
— *Gone with the Wind*

You can have whatever you want if you dress for it.
—Edith Head, Oscar-winning costume designer

Everyone cares what a woman wears. Every starlet walking the red carpet for the first time, every woman suddenly vaulted into the spotlight, every newly elected politician's wife quickly discovers that her wardrobe gets a lot of attention: sometimes positive but more often the negative type often referred to as *catty*.

Homo sapiens is one of the few species that emphasizes females' appearance more than males'. Male peacocks, cardinals, and ducks get the fabulous plumage; the females are drab brown, the better to sit, undetected, on their eggs. Lions sport gloriously long tresses; lionesses wear a crew cut. But humans? The males get to trot out the same suit or tux for every single party. In fact, when men go a little flamboyant with their evening attire, some people watchers savage them almost as brutally as they do women who take sartorial missteps. Females have the responsibility of looking flash, and with that responsibility comes some very difficult decisions: Black or red? Long or tea length? Sleeves or no sleeves? Gold or silver lamé?

Some women consider dressing one of the burdens of being female. For others, it's a sheer delight, one of the reasons they enjoy being a girl. That's Scarlett. She was born with great style and a love of clothes. In her carefree life as "the belle of five counties," as her father bragged, Scarlett spent nearly as many hours choosing her outfits as she did plotting to win Ashley Wilkes. Her anguishing over what to wear to the barbecue takes up nearly a full page, with pros and cons for each frock: color, cut, suitability, even condition (her favorite dress has a spot on it). It's a scene the movie portrayed beautifully, with a heap of colorful dresses piled on Scarlett's four-poster bed. Scarlett would be a Dolce & Gabbana girl today, showing off her figure in wildly patterned cut-to-there styles, with plenty of Bulgari to match.

Even as a widow, saddled with the burden of wearing stark black widow's weeds forever, Scarlett found a way to show her style. Simply put, she let Rhett Butler sway her with a green velvet bonnet from Paris. Once that bonnet was perched on her head, Scarlett flouted convention to wear the colors and styles she loved.

Today, Scarlett's taste for colorful fabrics and low-cut bodices, not to mention her gaudy engagement ring from Rhett, would most likely earn her a citation from E!'s Fashion Police, but she wouldn't care. Scarlett knew that a killer sense of style trumps beauty any day of the week.

Consider Sarah Jessica Parker. She's got great hair and a Pilates-perfect figure, but take away the makeup and the just-right clothes and she's hardly a conventional beauty. That hasn't stopped her from becoming a fashion icon, a woman whom designers love to dress and other women mimic at every high-heeled step. Parker's wardrobe choices, from where-did-you-*get*-that? necklaces to swingy ballet skirts to sky-high stilettos, have been so widely copied that, when *Sex and the City* ended, the fashion world was atwitter, trying madly to figure out who would replace her as the next small-screen style maven. Sarah Jessica Parker not beautiful? Tell that to the millions of women who'd love to have just one ounce of her impeccable sense of style.

Another famous example: Diana Vreeland, so plain her own mother called her "extremely ugly." Challenged by the insult, the Paris-born, Manhattan-bred Diana made the most of her trim figure and flair for fashion and wound up with the most glamorous job in the world, editor in chief of *Vogue*. From that perch, Vreeland dictated worldwide standards of beauty. She launched, and sank, the careers of dozens of women far more beautiful than she.

Women of style deserve a salute, especially in a world where so many women dress alike. The same why-on-earth-do-these-cost-two-hundred-dollars? jeans. The same barely there tops. The same Manolo Blahniks/Jimmy Choos or knockoffs. The same flouncy skirt, trench coat, or whatever happens to be on display in the window of Banana Republic. Even worse, the monotony of black, black, and more black, even in summer. "Is it possible that people could look so ugly?" the British designer Vivienne Westwood, a paragon of iconoclasm, once mused during a visit to the United States.

Better yet, stylish women should be studied. If there's a secret to their style, it's this: They know what they look good in, and no *Lucky* magazine layout will convince them otherwise. When Scarlett fretted over dresses for the barbecue, she rejected a lavender gown, "beautiful with those wide insets of lace and net about the hem," because it didn't suit her personality. She knew what worked for her and what didn't.

How did Scarlett, and how do other stylish women, know what works and what doesn't? As frightening as it sounds for the unstylish among us, these women *experiment* with clothes. They spend more money on fashion mistakes than timid dressers spend on their uniform-like wardrobes. Trial and error, either in the fitting room or on the street, leads to sartorial success.

These women also know what their best features are, and they buy clothes that play up those features. Remember Scarlett and her wardrobe of low-cut green dresses, which set off her eyes and her figure? Women who look in the mirror more than once a day know their strong suits: sexy shoulders, a tiny waist, a curvy butt. If you're not sure, ask your mother. She knows; she's been looking at you your whole life. And if your mother's not available, ask your oldest friend. (Don't ask your husband or boyfriend—*there's* an argument waiting to happen!)

Armed with your assets, go shopping, but do it differently. Visit an independent boutique, perhaps one you've avidly window-shopped but never set foot inside. If you can make the time, shop during the day on a weekday, when salespeople have more time to help you. And give yourself a fighting chance. The day you go shopping, wear underwear that works for your figure, not against it.

Speaking of underthings: They matter, especially bras. Take the time and trouble to get fitted for a bra, even if you're absolutely sure you're a 34B because that's what you've been your entire life. (Bosoms, like butts, tend to change position over time.) Spend money on that well-fitting bra, even if you only buy one and need to wash it by hand every single night. Even inexpensive clothes will look great if the body underneath them is well supported.

When you're shopping, try on clothes you've never considered before. Forget *I can't wear low-cut pants* or *I look a fright in orange*. Give them a chance. And look twice at clothes that appear unpromising on the hanger; stylish women know some of the clothes that look best on bodies look worst on hangers. Feel free to ask a saleswoman for her opinion, but let your gut make the final decision. If you feel luscious in an outfit, buy it and wear it.

Next, get your new outfit tailored to fit you perfectly. Unless you're the size of a "fit model," the woman whose proportions a designer cuts patterns for, clothes won't fit you perfectly right off the rack. Nor will the same size fit from store to store or from designer to designer. In fact, shopping will be a far saner experience if you ignore the size on the label. Size is just a number; the fit's the thing, which is why you should take your wardrobe staples—separates, dresses—to a good tailor and let her work magic with those straight pins.

Scarlett was lucky to be born in the pre-prefab world. All her dresses were custom-made from patterns drawn from her figure. Here's an idea: If your figure is hard to fit (long waist, long arms, whatever), why not have one suit custom-made? Custom's not as expensive as it sounds, considering the result: a one-of-a-kind garment that'll be the best-fitting thing you've ever worn. Much of the cost lies in the fabric, and there's plenty of fine, reasonably priced fabric to be found.

Finally, next time you go shopping, take Scarlett with you. She won't let you pass up that gorgeous sweater, the one that makes your skin glow but costs a bit more than you wanted to spend. She'll hand over your credit card for that slinky dress that seems to be lacking a few inches of fabric but makes you feel like a rock star. She'll stamp her foot and insist you buy that glamorous one-season jacket, partly because it's on sale (Scarlett was a thrifty girl) but mostly for the best reason of all: It makes you look like a million bucks.

LOOK LIKE A MOVIE STAR!

For the film *Gone with the Wind,* which debuted in 1939, costume designer Walter Plunkett brought Scarlett's wardrobe to life magnificently. From her prim flowered cotton dress in the first scene to the *va-va-va-voom* velvet gown she wore to Ashley's birthday party, Plunkett perfectly captured Scarlett's style and personality. Like Plunkett, today's costume designers have a flair for clothes and smart, creative ideas about how women should dress. Here's their silver-screen-to-real-life advice.

Don't think of clothes as fashion. "We're helping an actor create a character," says Daniel Orlandi, whose screen credits include *Down with Love,* starring Renée Zellweger. What a great idea! Think of yourself as a character and your life as a movie, and dress to match.

Fit is everything. Even expensive clothes look terrible if they don't fit. Spend the extra money for tailoring, even if it means buying fewer things.

Be comfortable. If an actress can't act in an uncomfortable costume, how can you live your life in one? Emotional comfort is important, too: "Sometimes you buy something that's fun, but it's not really you, and it sits in the closet," Orlandi says. "It's good to try new things and experiment, but you're going to be more confident if you're not thinking about your clothes."

Take it easy on the trends. As tempting as that hot-pink Chanel-style Target jacket looks, "Buy something you can keep for more than a season," advises Judianna Makovsky, costume designer for *Seabiscuit.* Makovsky buys good clothes (a cashmere V-neck sweater, a Prada jacket) and keeps them for "many, many, many years."

Simple is better. Colleen Atwood, whose credits include the movie version of *Chicago,* swears by a pared-down wardrobe that includes a "really good" black skirt, a well-fitting shirt and jacket, and black shoes that look good and feel comfortable.

Don't let your clothes wear you. "The focus should be on the person, not the clothes," says Makovsky. In fact, she loves it when people don't notice her work on the big screen. "That means the clothes are right."

Scarlett rule 3

RULES ARE MEANT TO BE BROKEN

"All you've done is to be different from other women and you've made a little success at it. As I've told you before, that is the one unforgivable sin in any society." —Rhett to Scarlett, *Gone with the Wind*

Any fool can make a rule, and any fool will mind it.

—Henry David Thoreau

Elizabeth Taylor has been married eight times. Elizabeth Hurley, who used to be known only as Hugh Grant's girlfriend, burst onto the scene decked out in a slinky Versace dress, just barely held together by safety pins. Anna Nicole Smith (née Vicki Lynn Hogan), the blond, busty ex-Guess model, married a Texas billionaire sixty-three years her senior—and persuaded a court to keep her in his will after his death. (Poor girl! Another court overturned the decision, but of course Anna's fighting it.)

Scandalous! How dare they. But people pay attention to, and secretly admire, women who do whatever the hell they want.

Scarlett did what *she* wanted, despite living in one of the most rule-bound societies ever to exist. In the prewar South, playing by the rules wasn't merely a good idea. It was practically law. Harsh consequences—exile from society in a world where society meant everything—awaited those who dared break the rules.

But Scarlett didn't care. She frequently—and gleefully—bent and broke those rules and even wrote a few of her own. In an era when a simple kiss was as good as a marriage proposal, Scarlett snuck one in here and another there. Shattering another rule of courtship, Scarlett told Ashley she loved him, not with a euphemism or flowery phrase but bluntly. And in the scene that sends chills up my spine whenever I read it, Scarlett snapped the chains of widowhood to lead the Virginia reel with Rhett Butler at the charity ball.

If Scarlett was so bent on breaking rules, to some extent it was because her lofty place in society tolerated it. Back then, as now, people were willing to overlook the bad behavior of members of rich, established families. Scarlett had a rule breaker's personality, too: She was a maverick, a me-first person—indeed, a pioneer—as were all the cotton growers of Clayton County, Georgia, a rugged hamlet far from the state's refined coastal cities. And Scarlett was a feminist, though our man-pleasing heroine would probably rather die than be labeled one.

Scarlett hated to be bored. A tomboy as a child, she carried that restless energy into adulthood. She couldn't be the kind of woman who sat quietly with a bit of embroidery in hand. She couldn't have borne to follow the well-worn path that women were expected to tread, moving from station to established station until the conveyor belt finally dumped her in the grave.

Of course, the war changed all that. It's hard to be bored when you don't know where your next meal is coming from.

It's not unreasonable to want to live safely, especially if you have kids. Plus, life usually throws enough curve balls to keep things interesting for most people.

The saying *Nothing ventured, nothing gained* is a dare or a challenge and not necessarily a positive one. After all, gains can be good or not so good. You can venture snowboarding and gain a broken leg, venture a stranger in a bar and gain an STD, venture a financial lark and gain a bankruptcy filing. But breaking a rule won't necessarily land you in the hospital or in a lawyer's office.

There are all kinds of rules to break. First, there are society's rules, the ones that exist so we all play together nicely, more or less. Stay in your lane while driving. Don't drive drunk. Put some clothes on before you go outside. Try not to kill anybody. Stay away from your neighbor's mate.

Then there are internal rules, the ones so drummed into you since childhood that they're part of your DNA. Attending the family's annual Fourth of July picnic. Brushing and flossing before bedtime. Shaking the orange-juice carton before pouring a glass. They're habits, done almost automatically.

Finally, there are life's unwritten rules, the kind most people play by because everyone else has and it's worked out for them. For example: Women aren't supposed to be aggressive. Assertive, perhaps; aggressive, no. Well, there's a rule Scarlett broke frequently and to great effect. From vowing to get Ashley to going into business, Scarlett showed an aggressive streak as fiery as Sherman's march through Georgia.

Here's another example: Women are responsible for the health of their relationships. Consider two real-life stories from the Sex and Relationships departments of two similar magazines: *Men's Fitness* and *Women's Health*. From the women's magazine: "IN THE TRENCHES. Is your relationship in a rut? Grab a shovel—we'll help dig you out." From the men's: "GET THE GIRL. How to keep her happy without committing." It looks like women are supposed to keep things lively in the love department, and men—well, when it gets dull, they move on.

Which rules are worth breaking? Probably not society's rules, those designed to help us live together safely and well. The consequences are scary and expensive and can wreck other people's lives, not to mention our own.

Unwritten rules are the most fun to break and have the biggest payoff. That one about women and aggression, for instance. Next time you and your friends go to a restaurant and they seat you in Siberia, that corner with a view of the bathrooms and the dirty-dish station, don't sit down. Stand up and tell the hostess or maître d' that you'd rather be somewhere more pleasant, perhaps at a table near a window or one with a garden view. If the answer's no, go somewhere else. That's what Scarlett would do. But the key isn't *asking;* asking is assertive. The key is *telling.* That's being aggressive. Scarlett would tell the waiter exactly which table she wanted—and she'd get it.

Look for opportunities to break small rules in daily life; they're everywhere. Take the elevator marked EMPLOYEES ONLY if it's the first one to open on your floor. Go up the DOWN escalator, especially in malls that place UP and DOWN escalators miles apart. Move to better seats at the opera house, concert hall, or movie theater after the first act (make sure the seats aren't already taken, or you'll be in the center of a most unpleasant ruckus).

Some rules are more difficult to break. Ending an awful, painful, unsalvageable marriage (yes, you've tried every idea *Woman's Day* ever printed) might mean a taboo second divorce, the ire of your family, and the loss of a few friends. Keeping your last name after you marry, if that's what you want to do, can draw raised eyebrows from your future mother-in-law, though you'd certainly qualify as a rule breaker: Only 1 percent of American women keep their birth names after they marry.

Rules don't have to be big to break. Sometimes it feels just as good to break the tiny ones. That might be why kids color outside the lines and dogs hop on the couch when nobody's home. The bottom line is this: If you're feeling hemmed in, step out of line, if only for a minute. You'll feel more in control, you'll feel more powerful, and, best of all, you'll have fun.

COURTLY MANNERS

Scarlett killed a man, stole a fiancé, and committed business fraud, but she never had to appear in court. Today it's a rare life that doesn't include at least one day in court: to defend a parking ticket, serve as a juror, support an accused family member, or, more seriously, stand as a defendant.

Court calls for manners that differ from those used in everyday life, says Dan Wolfe, president of the Baltimore-based American Society of Trial Consultants. Wolfe and his associates help attorneys make the most of their day in court; Wolfe has advice for the rest of us on how to do the same.

◆ Eating, drinking, and reading are not allowed in court, so load up on body and brain food before your appointed time.

◆ Leave your cell phone in the car. Some courts, including federal courts, will confiscate cell phones.

◆ Be clean and well groomed, "in clothing respectful of the court," Wolfe says. Many courts' websites post their dress code; if you're not sure, wear what passes as business attire in your area.

✦ Leave your hobbies at home. Even if you're a juror, knitting, crocheting, or other pastimes are not permissible; such activities deflect attention from the proceedings.

✦ If you're a defendant, take your lawyer's advice. "They want you to look good," Wolfe says. So if you hate navy blue but your lawyer tells you to wear a navy suit, do it.

Scarlett
rule 4

BLAZE A TRAIL

Go into business for herself! It was unthinkable.

—*Gone with the Wind*

Life is either a daring adventure or nothing at all.   —Helen Keller

"Y
ou go." "No, you first." "No, you." Every kid has had this conversation. It takes place at the edge of an untested swimming hole, at the foot of an unclimbed tree, at the entrance of an unexplored cave. Nobody wants to go first. Nobody wants to feel the shock of cold water, the dizzying height of the tree, the blank darkness of the cave.

But somebody's got to go first.

Scarlett went first, lots of times. From picking cotton and tilling the fields at Tara, work no gentle-bred Southern woman did, to taking over Frank Kennedy's store and lumber mill in Atlanta, Scarlett shoved conventions and even her darkest fears aside and took that first step.

Some trailblazers take their first steps for the good of humankind. Not Scarlett. Hers were selfish steps, taken out of desire or desperation and liberally laced with recklessness. She must have known how much was at stake—her reputation, her friendships, her standing in the community—as she stepped through the Virginia reel with Rhett, her somber black skirt swaying in time to the music. Still, she stepped through that reel, and when she was finished she danced another dance with Rhett, and then yet another. The other young women at the ball most likely noticed that it was possible to have fun *and* be a widow without stopping the earth, but Scarlett wasn't waltzing to be a role model. She simply wanted to dance.

When Scarlett was running Frank's store and lumber mills, she flaunted her pregnancy in public. Pregnancy as a secret or shameful thing is a laughable concept today, when women wear stretch tops to show off their swelling bellies and gossip magazines keep track of celebrity "bumps." But in Scarlett's day, the word *pregnant* wasn't spoken, and women went into hiding for *confinements*.

Privately, Scarlett was probably as mortified as the genteel folk who witnessed her shocking breach of propriety, but in her mind she simply had no choice. She had a business to run, and pregnancy just couldn't stand in the way.

Commandeering the mills and the store was yet another first step Scarlett took out of necessity. She could have sold needlework or, like her neighbor, Mrs. Merriwether, peddled pies for a living, both acceptable occupations for women who were forced by the circumstances of war to earn a living. But Scarlett didn't want just enough money to subsist on. She wanted lots of it, and the best way to rake in piles of cash was in the exclusively male worlds of commerce and construction.

Isn't that the way it often is with trailblazers and trendsetters? How often do they announce: *I intend to take this first step so that other women may do likewise*? Most trailblazing men and women have their own desires and needs to fulfill and rarely act on behalf of a whole gender. Consider George Mallory's answer when someone asked him why he wanted to climb Mount Everest: "Because it's there."

It takes balls, as men love to say, to go first. She who takes the first step doesn't know what she's getting into. That swimming hole could be numbingly cold or full of algae. And she who takes the first step is usually responsible for the second step, too, even if the first wasn't a whole lot of fun.

First steps, whether for an individual or for the entire planet, are scary because the outcome's a mystery. Will you be laughed at? Escorted out of the building? Succeed? Fail? Seasoned first steppers like Scarlett know not to be afraid, especially of failure. Any successful businesswoman will swear that failure is a far better teacher than success.

Trailblazing doesn't have to be dramatic and world-changing to be worthwhile and effective. Everyday life offers plenty of chances to blaze tiny trails, paths that strengthen relationships and communities. At the next meeting you attend, be the first to raise your hand to volunteer for a project. If there's litter on your street, be the first to grab a pair of gloves and a plastic bag and pick it up.

When you're at a book club meeting, be the first to offer an opinion on the book—and make it a big, bold opinion. The other members will be grateful that you blazed this particular trail. (While you're at it, be first to take one of those home-made brownies from the plate.) Be the first to pick up the phone to rekindle an old friendship. You haven't heard from her in ages? Guess what: She hasn't heard from you, either.

Be the first to end an argument with a friend, spouse, or sibling. Certainly Scarlett's go-first attitude failed her here: Had she been first to end the long-simmering war of one-upmanship with Rhett, he might not have left her with that withering "I don't give a damn" ringing in her ears.

Be the first to say I'm sorry, even if you're 100 percent positive you didn't do anything wrong and especially if the argument's about something stupid (and isn't that true of 99 percent of arguments?). You'll feel good taking that step, and you'll have paved the way for the other party (spouse, partner, mother-in-law, sister, whoever) to take it the next time.

If you want to take a *big* first step, one that resonates be-yond your front door, consider the issues you're passionate about. Does a busy intersection need a stop sign or traffic sig-nal? Is there a health issue that you think demands more attention—and money? Melissa Zagon did. In her early thir-ties, Zagon, an attorney with a young daughter, was diag-nosed with lung cancer. When Zagon discovered that lung cancer research was underfunded compared with research for other cancers, she and several of her fellow patients launched LUNGevity Foundation. Five years later, it was the country's largest private supporter of lung cancer research; in 2005, the organization raised more than two million dollars.

Go first. Pick up the phone and call the mayor or alderman or whoever gets things done in your city. It might take forever—after all, American women fought seventy-two years for the right to vote—and you might have to retire from the battle before the mission is accomplished. But you'll be able to rest in peace, knowing that you started something. People will remember your efforts; you might even get a park bench named in your honor.

First steps have a domino effect. One person raises her hand or offers an opinion, and soon everyone's doing it. But whoever does it first gets bragging rights, an incomparable sense of pride, and a much more satisfying life. As Scarlett knew, only the lead dog gets a change of scenery.

SURVIVING THE SPOTLIGHT

Scarlett lived before the age of mass media, before reporters swarmed around the slightest scent of a story. She never had to worry about what to wear on TV or what to say to an inquisitive interviewer. Today, chances are good that if you blaze a trail, or if you even end up in the wake of a trailblazer, some reporter will call you to talk about it.

There's an art to handling the media, says Eileen Michaels, president of Adison Inc., a New York public relations firm that specializes in media communications. When Michaels preps her clients for media appearances, here's what she suggests.

Wardrobe. Choose gray, navy, or beige instead of black, which looks too severe on camera. Avoid lace, ruffles, or small prints. "You don't want to look cutesy," Michaels says. Wear a bra, even if you usually don't.

Jewelry. Avoid shiny or dangling jewelry. Pearl earrings (pierced or clip-on) are smart because they frame your face.

Makeup. Let the makeup person redo your face. She knows what looks best on camera.

Posture. On camera, sit with your legs crossed at the ankles and with your feet on the floor. Roll your shoulders and sit straight but avoid a forced look. If you're wearing a jacket, sit on it to prevent the shoulders from bunching up.

Poise. Keep your arms in an open gesture, not folded, and don't clench your fists. Put your hands in your lap or hang them loosely at your sides.

Focus. Don't keep your focus solely on either the camera or the interviewer. Look at the interviewer when she asks you a question, but turn to the camera when you answer, because that's where your audience is.

Questions. Get as much information about the direction of the interview beforehand as you can, to prevent surprises. During the interview, never say *I don't want to answer that* or *No comment.* If you're asked an awkward question, reply with, "That's a good question, Barbara," and then say what you want to say.

TV crews. When you're approached on the street, don't be sensational. Make your answers brief and concise, and don't move around a lot or gesture wildly. Remember, if you don't want to be on TV, you don't have to. "Tell the reporter you'd rather not be on the air and don't give your name," Michaels suggests.

Scarlett
rule 5

BE YOURSELF

There was no one to tell Scarlett that her own personality, frighteningly vital though it was, was more attractive than any masquerade she might adopt.
—Gone with the Wind

I'm not like anyone. I'm me.
—Elizabeth Taylor

Like a lot of girls, Scarlett wanted to grow up to be just like her mother. And no wonder. Gentle and kind, efficient yet never brusque, effective but never forceful, Ellen Robillard O'Hara embodied the perfect plantation owner's wife and, therefore, the perfect Southern woman. On the outside, she was soft cotton, an ethereal creature of delicacy and good breeding. Inside, she was cast iron, able to weather all sorts of adversity without mussing her chignon.

Scarlett wasn't like her mother. She wasn't like Melanie Hamilton. Nor was she like India and Honey Wilkes, Maybelle Merriwether, or the other girls her age, all of whom were more than willing to hide their real personalities behind the veneer of manners and breeding so prized in the South.

This veneer rarely cracked, at least not in public. Ashley's sisters, India and Honey, and the other young women who would have been Scarlett's friends—if she had had any female friends—never told Scarlett exactly what they thought of her high spirits and vivacious ways, which had a way of attracting their beaux to Scarlett's side. The veneer cracked only when tempers bubbled beyond the boiling point, as India Wilkes's did the night Frank Kennedy was killed while on a mission to avenge Scarlett's honor.

Scarlett was as carefully brought up as her peers and keenly aware that well-mannered women and chivalrous men fueled Southern society just as slave labor and cotton stoked its economy. But Scarlett couldn't manage to keep the lid on her volcanic personality. She knew what not to say and what not to do. But she said and did them anyway.

It wasn't difficult for Scarlett to be herself, but she found it tough to accept herself as she was. The memory of Ellen grated incessantly against the reality of Scarlett: gentle lady versus grabby girl, devoted wife versus serial widow, rule follower versus rule breaker. Every single day reminded Scarlett that she was not a great lady and most likely would never be one.

To feel more comfortable, Scarlett summoned her never-failing charm—"I'll think about that tomorrow"—and told herself she'd become more like Ellen after she was rich. After she had restored Tara to its pristine beauty. After she had wrested Ashley away from Melanie.

But the charm only lasted so long. Scarlett didn't discover inner peace until she finally put Ellen's saintly ghost to rest and realized she was not her mother and never would be. Alas, Scarlett stumbled on the truth a little too late.

As Scarlett in her costume of hoopskirts and corset knew all too well, being yourself has hardly anything to do with hair, makeup, or clothes. Oh sure, some people use their appearance to be different: wildly colored hair, tattoos, piercings, eccentric clothes. But elaborate ink, metal, and fabric adornments don't mean much anymore. So many people have a tattooed or pierced something that tattoos and piercings are hardly a mark of individuality; it's more unusual to be tattoo-free, with no human-made holes anywhere.

The way to be yourself is just to *be* yourself. Do what makes you happy. Desire a husband, a child, a new car, a pair of expensive jeans, or whatever not because all your friends have one but because it truly meets your inner needs. Avoid situations that produce an uncomfortable tug in your gut.

Being comfortable in their own skin is easy enough for some women, those born with perfectly calibrated inner compasses. They're enviably self-possessed. They know what they want almost from the day they're born. If they ever misstep, you don't see it. If they ever doubt themselves, you don't hear about it.

Late bloomers don't have it so easy. They experiment for a year (or a decade) or two, cycling through a dizzying array of personae—hippie chick, arty coffeehouse gal, sexpot, driven career woman—before they happen on their true self. There's an upside to such inner mayhem: These women usually have interesting closets and a fascinating collection of friends.

Like Scarlett, some women are well aware of—and entirely frustrated by—their true selves, so they try to change. The quiet girl morphs into the life-of-the-party barfly. The smart girl plays dumb for a while. Whoever first said "What's a girl like you doing in a place like this?" was probably talking to one of these works-in-progress.

For almost everybody, it takes time to realize that, while imitation might be the sincerest form of flattery, it's also the straightest route to unhappiness. Ask any high school girl who's put on makeup, tight jeans, and a tiny top to fit in with the "popular" crowd. What happens? The popular girls see right through the facade, her old friends dump her for being a traitor, and she ends up sitting home alone with a bag of Doritos on Friday night.

Don't compare yourself and your life with your friends and their lives. It's tough not to look at a college friend and say, "She's got two kids and a house in the suburbs, and I'm sitting alone in this crummy sublet." Her life is hers. Yours is yours. For all you know, she envies your freedom. On the flip side, don't feel smug about the former dorm mate who's selling shoes at Sears while you're a vice president at the city's biggest marketing firm. She may sleep better at night than you do.

Another path to self-contentment: Indulge in activities that let you be you. Love animals? Volunteer at a shelter. Does cooking nourish your soul? Throw dinner parties for your friends. If dancing's your passion but life didn't lead you to the

Joffrey Ballet's doorstep, take dance lessons. And the flip side again: If you're not a party girl, don't hang out at bars with party-girl friends. Make a date to see them for lunch or coffee instead.

No life is without its awkward moments, the kind that make you want the earth to open up and swallow you whole. Being yourself and accepting that self, warts and all, will let you toss off those moments and move on. Despite its sad ending, with Bonnie's death and Rhett's departure, one of the triumphs of *Gone with the Wind* is Scarlett's willingness to let Scarlett be Scarlett. Will she win Rhett back? I'd say yes, with that sublime self-acceptance as her sharpest tool.

Scarlett lesson

LOVE YOUR QUIRKS

Scarlett, nothing if not an iconoclast, couldn't help but be herself. Being different was a challenge for her.

It's a challenge today, too, though hardly an insurmountable one. Even as a child, Wendy McClure, author of *I'm Not the New Me* (Riverhead Books, 2005), a witty, keenly observant memoir, had a different sort of outlook on life, but it's served her well in her career as a writer and blogger. McClure shares a few tips on how to be different in a homogeneous world.

✦ Remember that you're not alone. "Everybody likes to think they have a quirk."

✦ Get over yourself. Chances are good that other people don't even notice the quirks that you think stick out like a pink Mohawk. "It's a very funny thing to think that what sets you apart doesn't even occur to some people," McClure says.

✦ Recognize your own comfort level. Make friends with people who like you for who you are; don't try to be who you aren't.

✦ Don't blame difficulties on your quirks. If you find yourself constantly battling the world, there's probably something more going on than your personality.

✦ Accept yourself and your idiosyncrasies. "You are who you are for a reason," McClure says.

Scarlett rule 6

SWEAR IF YOU FEEL LIKE IT

"They are damn Yankees!" cried Scarlett passionately.

—Gone with the Wind

Ever notice that "What the hell" is always the right decision?

—Marilyn Monroe

In Scarlett's day, Southern women didn't talk as much as murmur. They spoke softly and carefully, choosing words that never provoked or harmed. The art of gentle speech was so hammered into girls that Scarlett, burning with fury over Ashley's rejection of her, couldn't summon a devastating word to call him. *Cad* was the worst she could think of, and Ashley was gentleman enough to turn white at the sound of it. But not Rhett: He wouldn't wither, not even at the worst polite words Scarlett hurled at him.

Scarlett's speech grew less careful as she got older. She borrowed one of her favorite cut-loose phrases from Gerald, her Irish father who, like Scarlett, hid a scrappy rogue's personality under a veneer of gentility. "God's nightgown!" Gerald would bellow when his temper flared or the world didn't go quite his way—and, in time, so did Scarlett. *Damn*, part of everyday discourse today but positively conversation-stopping back then, was another favorite of Scarlett's, especially when applied to Yankees.

Today, it's almost impossible to walk by a group of people, men or women, without hearing at least one jarring word, be it *hell, damn, shit*, or even *fuck*, uttered in the course of normal everyday conversation. *Fuck* has become such a common word that it's become an "infix"—a part of speech nestled inside of a word, rather than at the beginning, as a prefix, or at the end, as a suffix. The examples linguists love to use? *Fan-fucking-tastic* and *un-fucking-believable*. It's amazing how creative we can be with language.

Creative and yet lacking in creativity. The rap on swearing is this: People use rough language because they have poor vocabularies. They're not educated enough to pull a devastating and yet socially acceptable phrase out of the hat, so they choose the lowest common denominator, a four-letter word or perhaps several of them linked together.

Swearwords used to be powerful in polite society, not just

because they sound short and punchy, like aural jabs in the air, but because they were used so sparingly. Swearing commanded attention when other words failed. *This is business!* a swearword announced. *The gloves are off. Bitch* could start a catfight; *fuck you* could lead to a broken bottle smashed over the head. Now some women use *bitch* as a term of endearment, and younger women, in search of more provocative linguistic territory, are trading up, as it were, to a new bad word—*cunt*—which still stops conversation in some circles, but perhaps not for much longer.

Polite public conversation, free of rough language, might be on its way to hell in a handbasket. But within individual vocabularies, swearwords can still pack tremendous power. A woman who never swears and rarely loses her temper will quite assuredly attract attention when she drops an *f-* or an *s-*bomb. The title of this chapter says it all: Swear if you feel like it. During an argument, when your opponent refuses to listen no matter how persuasive your language, drop a single swearword.

Swearing is especially effective when you're arguing with a man. Men don't listen when another man swears—it's like a bird chirping or a dog barking—but when a woman swears, they take notice. It's like a bird barking or a dog chirping: totally unexpected.

Here's another time you should swear: When you're alone, and you're frustrated by a task that just won't get done or a miles-long to-do list and only twenty-four hours in the day, or you've suddenly gotten bad news. A string of swearwords—the more creative, the better—lets off steam like a fast run around the block. Swearing isn't like that mythical tree in the forest. If you swear, and nobody's around to hear it, it's still swearing, and it's still satisfying.

Swearing's a right-time right-place proposition. There are times and places when swearing is probably not wise: when you're stopped by a traffic cop, for example. And don't swear when you're lodging a complaint with a service company. Some companies, wanting to protect their employees from indelicate language, instruct telephone representatives to hang up on swearing customers.

You probably shouldn't swear at work, even if everyone else does, from your boss right on down to the mail clerk, even if your office sports an every-day-is-casual-Friday attitude. At least don't swear in the coffee room or at the watercooler. But if you're having an intense (and private) discussion with your boss, and she drops the first swearword, why not follow suit? If she's speaking inappropriately, no reason you can't, too, if for no other purpose than to send a message.

Scarlett said what bubbled to her lips, consequences be damned, so she swore more than the average gentlewoman. Still, she saved the heavy verbal artillery the way some women save a drop-dead outfit or a bottle of expensive perfume. Trotted out infrequently, on just the right occasion, a swearword is killer.

WHEN SWEARING'S NOT AN OPTION

Scarlett knew, even if her anger bubbled over, that certain venues and situations were not appropriate for swearing, and that's true even in today's cuss-tolerant culture. When every fiber of your being wants to swear, but you know you shouldn't, here's what to do, according to W. Robert Nay, author of *Taking Charge of Anger: How to Resolve Conflict, Sustain Relationships, and Express Yourself Without Losing Control* (Guilford Press, 2003).

1. Sit down. Angry people usually leap to their feet, a move that fuels anger and emits a message of defensiveness. Sitting tells your brain—and other people—that you're in control. "Your body position is important in regulating how you feel and how others interpret you," Nay says.

2. Learn your anger cues. Hot face? Pounding heart? Shaky legs? When you know you're about to go ballistic, "Say *stop* forcefully in your head," Nay suggests.

3. Take a deep breath and count down from ten to one. Deep breathing and counting throw a wet blanket on the brain's arousal to anger.

4. Figure out why you're so angry. Don't leap to conclusions; don't automatically take the situation personally. "Look at it through a clear lens," Nay advises. And if you need time to think, ask to go to the bathroom. "Nobody's going to tell you that you can't go to the bathroom."

5. Decide what you need to end the angry situation and request it politely.

6. Express your needs in terms of *I*, not *you*. *I felt slighted when you interrupted me* is more effective than *Why did you interrupt me?* Nay explains.

7. Rehearse these techniques. Mildly annoying situations, such as a slow line in a grocery store or a snotty store clerk, provide good practice situations.

8. Don't worry about memorizing all these steps. "If clients get twenty-five percent of what I say, they'll do fine," Nay says.

Scarlett
rule 7

The moss green velvet curtains felt prickly and soft beneath her cheek. . . . And then suddenly she looked at them.

—*Gone with the Wind*

The true sign of intelligence is not knowledge but imagination.

—Albert Einstein

What is it about curtains and strong women? Scarlett tore down her mother's prized drapes to make not just any old dress but the dress that saved Tara from the tax collectors. In *The Sound of Music*, Maria refashions some cotton curtains into play clothes for the von Trapp children, in a move that first vexes but ultimately charms their stony father into falling in love with her.

Of course it's not the curtains but the ingenuity of looking at a window covering and seeing a fancy dress or a passel of play clothes. Scarlett might have dropped out of finishing school, but she had a good head on her shoulders and resourceful genes she inherited from her successful immigrant father.

Throughout her story, Scarlett relied on her brains and resourcefulness to maneuver out of a number of jams. The curtain scene tops the list. Mention *Gone with the Wind* and that scene from the movie pops to mind. And, for those of a certain generation, so does Carol Burnett's parody of that scene, in which she models not only the curtains but the curtain rod and rings, too.

Examples abound: At the barbecue, Scarlett sat so as to surround herself with admirers, and when Sherman's army showed up on her doorstep, she shoved a wallet containing all the money she owned into Melanie's baby's diaper. Some of Scarlett's resourceful moves were a little unsavory—for instance, stealing Suellen's fiancé—but Scarlett didn't care. For her, the end always justified the means.

Your skirt hem unravels before a big presentation. Your red-hot date cancels three hours before the party. The in-laws have stopped by, unannounced, and all you've got in the way of snacks is a can of Sprite and a bag of stale pretzels. Those wonderful relationship-strengthening therapy sessions are instead suddenly proving that the marriage *can't* be saved.

It's a rare woman whose life doesn't surprise her with a "Great; now what?" once in a while.

It's easy to say, like a Girl Scout, *Be prepared.* Check the hem of your skirt the night before, be willing and able to go to a big party alone, always have a can of nuts in the freezer and a bottle of wine in the fridge should company show up at the door, and for God's sake don't marry the wrong guy. But that's like telling Scarlett she should have packed away one of her dozens of dresses in the cellar at Tara, "just in case." Martha Stewart and other perfectly organized women with television shows always seem to plan ahead. Normal women with normal lives don't. Reality gets in the way.

When Scarlett turned that green velvet from drapery to dress, our finishing-school dropout probably didn't realize she was carrying out a textbook—or shall we say novel—approach to problem solving. Here's what Scarlett did and why it worked:

She stayed focused

Scarlett didn't pine for a whole wardrobe of new clothes but limited her wish to a single pretty dress. Problems, even tiny nagging ones, have a nasty way of growing into one gigantic "my life is horrible and I'm going to jump off a bridge" mess. Scarlett didn't let herself get dialed up. She decided specifically what she wanted, and she kept calm. She was a little dejected, to be sure, but calm.

She looked for a change of scenery

When mulling the dress problem, Scarlett was sitting in Tara's parlor, which had been transformed into a dark, gloomy sick-room for dozens of soldiers. Longing for the smells and sight of the land she loved so much, Scarlett rose from her chair to open the curtains and the windows. Had she simply sat there in the dark, she never would have given that green velvet a second look.

The takeaway? When you're stuck on a problem, change direction. Get up from your office chair. Take a walk. Page through a newspaper or magazine. Sort through that pile of junk mail. Open a drawer, a cabinet, or a closet. With a little time and a little searching outside the box, who knows what brilliant solution you'll stumble upon?

She didn't look a gift horse in the mouth

Scarlett allowed the curtains to be her solution. She didn't pooh-pooh them for being heavy velvet, a little worn out and covered with dust; she didn't wish they were pristine French-made watered silk instead. When Scarlett found her solution, she didn't waste time with second-guessing. She let the solution be the solution.

She didn't let opposition stop her

When Mammy protested Scarlett's plan, Scarlett persisted. If a solution works for you, refuse to take no for an answer. And in difficult situations—say, a divorce or leaving a relationship—you might have to hold on tight to your decision. Dissenters, those who would rather have you wallow in your problem than be free of it, can emerge from the most surprising corners.

No life, even the life of your most successful friend, marches along free of problems. The small ones are annoying; bigger dilemmas can be terrifying, even immobilizing. But if you find yourself with a problem and no solution in sight, keep calm and keep looking. If Scarlett, a sixteen-year-old with no formal education, could do it, so can you. Sometimes the answer to even the most vexing problem is in plain sight. Just keep your eyes open—and find it.

UNLEASH YOUR CREATIVITY

Scarlett had a distinct creative advantage: "Her back was pushed against the wall," says Maureen Shirreff, longtime ad-woman and one of the creators of Dove's provocative Campaign for Real Beauty, which features everyday women instead of actors or models. Says Shirreff, "By hook or by crook, those kinds of people figure out how to get what they want."

For less desperate times that still call for top-notch creative thinking, Shirreff passes along these tricks for jump-starting your brain.

Reinforce your creative self. Explore your garden, your closet, your jewelry box; cuddle with your children, if they represent your supreme expression of creativity. Such reinforcement says, "Yes, I do have a creative self," according to Shirreff. Plus, exploring familiar territory "is like being a little kid again—it blocks out the world."

Know what inspires you. Fill a scrapbook or manila folder with ads, photos, magazine covers, or kids' drawings that make you positively shiver with delight.

Explore the unfamiliar. If you love rock-and-roll, put on some Mozart or hip-hop. If you adore Renoir, page through a book of Kandinsky paintings or Cartier-Bresson photographs. "You never know what you might find," Shirreff says.

Work with your opposite hand. Giving your nondominant hand a chance to write, draw, or even open a can of soup exercises the nondominant half of your brain, which can unleash a flood of creativity. Shirreff, a right-handed painter, finds that she "sees" better when she draws with her left hand.

Revert to your childhood. When she's stuck, Shirreff pages through fairy-tale books illustrated by Tasha Tudor, the same books she treasured as a child. The familiar beauty of the books comforts her—and jump-starts her creativity.

Don't be afraid of creativity. And don't overthink it. "Creativity should be delightful, not painful," Shirreff says of the creative process. "I really think we make things harder for ourselves."

Scarlett
rule 8

KEEP YOUR EYES ON THE PRIZE

"I'm never going to be hungry again."   —Scarlett, *Gone with the Wind*

I have a woman's ability to stick to a job and get on with it when
everyone else walks off and leaves it.
                                                    —Margaret Thatcher

Scarlett's feverish ambitions—to win Ashley, to never be
hungry again, to persuade Rhett back to her side—drive
the plot of *Gone with the Wind* from its idyllic beginning to its
bittersweet conclusion.

Scarcely a dozen pages go by without Scarlett making her
first vow—to persuade Ashley to marry *her*, not his cousin
Melanie. Planning and scheming for Ashley possessed Scarlett
from the moment the Tarleton twins told her the news of
Ashley's engagement to the second she ambushed Ashley in

the library. The thought of failure merely flitted through her mind.

Scarlett's second goal—never to be hungry again—is hardly trifling and even more daunting. She couldn't possibly have known that she would have to steal and kill to meet that goal.

Scarlett's third goal, the novel's cliff-hanger? Get Rhett. Her third husband abandoned her and her glamorously tacky house mere hours after Scarlett realized he was the love of her life.

As Scarlett sat on her steps, watching Rhett walk out the door, she was two for three in the goal department. Ashley was hers, thanks to Melanie's death. She was one of the richest and best-fed women in Atlanta, able to say what she wanted and do what she wanted and not care about what people thought, as she vowed to Mammy the day of the Wilkeses' barbecue.

Nobody ever accused Scarlett O'Hara of being perfect, and her attitude toward her goals illustrates her imperfections all too painfully; she allowed them to govern her life rather than guide it. And she had a habit of setting aside morals to meet those goals. At the end of her story, rich with money and possessions but bereft of both Rhett and her old friends, even Scarlett realized that the price she paid to reach her goals was far too high.

Setting a goal can be as vague and fluttery as Scarlett's aunt Pittypat or as strong and decisive as Rhett. "Get in shape" is a Pittypat goal; "Be able to run two miles" is a Rhett goal. "Get promoted" is Pittypat; "Become vice president of sales" is more like Rhett.

That's the first rule of goal-reaching: Be specific about where you want to go, not vague. Why? Specific goals demand a plan, with particular steps taken along a particular path, while vague goals don't. That sales job, for instance, requires gaining experience in the sales department, while "getting promoted" doesn't point in any real direction.

The second rule: Set a time frame. If you are determined to reach a goal, setting an end date will add a sense of urgency, a realization that the clock is ticking so you had better start working right away. Set mini-goals within that time frame, all stretching toward the big one. Life coaches call them *baby steps*. For example, if you want to learn to cook, don't start with a Cordon Bleu recipe. Learn the basics and then move on to more complicated dishes.

The third rule of goals: Be reasonable. So many goals are abandoned by the wayside because they were, from the start, unattainable.

There's a fourth rule: Be flexible. As you progress, you might discover that your timetable is off kilter or that your original goal is unmanageable.

Scarlett O'Hara might have gone a little overboard with ambition. She might have let goals run her life, and she might have taken a few regrettable steps to meet them. But the uneducated Scarlett, a woman in a man's world, got what she wanted. With just a fraction of Scarlett's guts and drive, other women can do the same.

BABY STEPS WILL TAKE YOU EVERYWHERE

Lynn Robinson, a Boston-based life coach and author of *Divine Intuition* (DK Publishing, 2001), saw *Gone with the Wind* as a girl and remembers feeling inspired by Scarlett. "She had so much spirit and creativity and ability to go for what she wanted," Robinson says. Scarlett took baby steps to reach her goals simply out of necessity, but it's always a marvelous idea to break a big goal into small steps. Robinson tells how.

Be specific. As we saw, vague statements such as "I want a promotion" or "I want to feel better" aren't energizing or engaging. However, a specific statement—"I want to weigh 135 pounds and feel great about my body"—is "juicy," Robinson says. "Put some strong feelings into your goals to make them exciting and worth going for."

Do your research. For instance, if you plan to run a marathon, read some magazine articles about it. Investigate hiring a personal trainer. Talk to people who have run a race. Reading and talking might seem like procrastination, but "It's crucial," Robinson says. "It gets the goal out of *I can't do it* to *Yes, I can.*"

Break your goal into doable steps. You won't be able to organize your entire house in one day, but you can clear off the top of a file cabinet, clean out a drawer, or organize half of a closet. "When we make goals too big, we don't see progress," Robinson says.

Keep a list of your accomplishments. Write them down and review them every day; if you don't, your progress will seem invisible.

Fight discouragement. Instead of bemoaning how far you have to go, celebrate how far you've come, Robinson advises. "Look for evidence that the goal is happening": a cleaner office, a trimmer figure, a fabulous résumé, and three great job interviews.

Reward yourself. When you accomplish a mini-goal—be it running two miles straight or cleaning out a complete closet—treat yourself to a little something special. Rewards double as motivation.

Listen to yourself. As you're working toward your goal, be open to changing it. "Intuition might tell you that a smaller goal is in order"—for instance, a 10K race instead of a marathon. "I'm a big fan of asking your intuition: *What's the best way?*" Robinson says.

Scarlett
rule 9

JUST DO IT

It was going to be difficult, telling Melanie that she and Prissy were to deliver her baby. —Gone with the Wind

You must do the thing you think you cannot do. —Eleanor Roosevelt

Every so often, you read about someone acting heroically in unbelievable circumstances. A woman hoists a three-thousand-pound car to free a child trapped underneath. A firefighter dashes into a burning house to save the family dog. A hostage makes pancakes for a would-be mass murderer and, thanks to her patient ministrations, he surrenders to the police.

The first reaction to these stories: *Wow!* The second: *What were they thinking?* And the answer to that: *Probably not much at all.* Had those heroes taken the time to think through their actions, the car would have been dropped, the family dog would be toast, and the mass murderer would have taken more victims.

Scarlett's hoopskirted figure has been fashioned into a book of paper dolls, but she would have made a great 3-D action figure, complete with movable limbs and a voice box packed with key phrases: "Fiddle dee dee!" . . . "Oh, Ashley!" Scarlett O'Hara was nothing if not a take-action gal. She was not one to sit still, waiting patiently for her life to happen. She would rather make any move, even a wrong one, than sit back and wait for life to run its course. It was, at once, one of her greatest weaknesses and one of her greatest strengths.

Impetuousness sometimes pushed Scarlett into bad decisions: for instance, luring Charles Hamilton into marrying her, the result being perhaps the worst marriage match in all of Clayton County. Scarlett's urge to act often overcame common sense, as it did when she insisted on leaving Atlanta for Tara even though the war was raging outside her front door.

Scarlett's go-go nature helped her keep the Union Army from destroying Tara, not once but twice. It let her deliver Melanie's baby, even though she was a sheltered teenager who could scarcely tie a bandage, much less an umbilical cord. It helped her shoulder the responsibility to feed, clothe, and shelter her entire family, work the fields of Tara to help restore at least some of its vitality, and turn Frank's store and the lumber mills from money losers into moneymakers.

One reason Scarlett was always able to act is that she always had a Plan B. Rarely did she sit and stew when her first course of action failed; her nimble brain would devise a second solution seemingly on the spot, especially when she spied an opportunity. And Scarlett always kept her eyes open for opportunities. When Rhett, languishing in jail, was unable to lend her tax money for Tara, she spied an opportunity in her sister's well-off shopkeeper fiancé—and got the money from him instead.

A regrettable move? Perhaps. But had Scarlett been able to turn back time, she wouldn't have changed a thing. Scarlett wasn't born to wait and watch, she was born to act.

It's wise to consider courses of action carefully when the outcome will affect friends, family, and others whose lives intersect with yours. Major purchases, job changes, moves, marriage, and divorce deserve at least a modicum of thought, maybe even that time-honored exercise of getting a sheet of paper, writing PRO on one side and CON on the other, and then filling in the columns.

The thing is, when all the pros and cons are written down and counted up, doesn't it seem that no matter which side has more entries, or which outcome seems more reasonable on paper, you end up going with your gut instead? That's what *Just do it* is all about: acting quickly, letting your instincts take over, and, above all, not thinking a situation practically to death. Overthinking is the mental equivalent of tearing up a paper napkin. First you've got halves, then you've got quarters, then you've got confetti, and finally all you've got is a linty mess that's not only useless but impossible to reconstruct.

Just do it applies to many situations in life, both simple and complicated. In traffic, you can't sit around debating whether to motor on through a yellow light or whether to make a quick left turn. You need to just do it, before the light turns red or oncoming traffic threatens to broadside you. Career maintenance sometimes requires lightning-quick action: dropping everything to apply for that dream job or volunteering for a high-profile assignment before your archrival does.

Relationships sometimes cry out for quick action. Waiting forever to find out if Mr. Okay's going to morph into Mr. Right only wastes precious time; sometimes you just have to take action. No matter how good he looks on paper, no matter how many qualities you list on the PRO side of the notebook, if your gut tells you he's not The One, cut him loose and begin the search for the guy you'll be happy with forever and then some.

A quick thinker embraces spontaneity whenever the opportunity arises. She's all for a girlfriend's invitation for a midday cup of coffee, a child's suggestion to take an after-school bike ride, a husband's offer of a late-night stroll. She doesn't say *but I have to . . .* and she doesn't fret about dinner or the laundry or the bathtub grout. She knows that the best moments are spontaneous ones and that spontaneity yields undreamed-of opportunities, not to mention some of life's sweetest memories.

A just-do-it woman realizes that it's useful to mull over a problem, but she knows just as certainly that too much thinking wastes time. Few problems come saddled with unlimited facets requiring infinite pondering. When she's stuck, she might resort to a mental version of the pros-and-cons list, but she makes it snappy and then makes a decision.

Just-do-it types don't saddle themselves with excuses not to approach a different task. Most important, they never say *I can't*. They know that phrase means the death of any endeavor. It means failure. It means quitting. So whether they're finding a place on a map or reading the instructions for how to assemble a new bookshelf from Ikea, their catchphrase is far more useful. It's *How can I?*

Just-do-it women tackle distasteful tasks sooner rather than later, the better to get them out of the way and move on to more entertaining adventures. They also know that, while time may heal all wounds, it doesn't solve all problems; it can make them worse. So rather than give their husbands the silent treatment when they're fighting or ignore their mothers' phone calls when they've had a disagreement, they tackle tough situations head-on and get them out of the way.

When it comes to the most heart-wrenching situations life has to offer—death, divorce, waiting for what is sure to be bad news—just-do-it women arm themselves with experience. They reach into their pasts for the most awful thing they ever dealt with and then set a bar: If I could do that, I can do anything. Scarlett's threshold for emotional pain was murdering the Yankee soldier. Everyone has an "it can't get worse than this" moment in her life: losing a parent, getting fired, enduring a horrid illness. Next time you're in a move-or-die situation, remember that worst time of your life and think like Scarlett.

For better or for worse, Scarlett rarely wasted time weighing every facet of the dozens of decisions she made. She thought quickly, acted quickly, and when she was wrong she didn't waste time bemoaning her situation; she moved on. If Nike were around during Scarlett's time, she'd have worn cross trainers, not those delicate Moroccan slippers. *Just do it* would have been her motto. Why not make it yours?

Scarlett lesson

THINK FAST

Gone with the Wind fan Jim Camp knows why Scarlett was able to make decisions so quickly. "She had amazing vision. She knew who she was and what she wanted her life to look like," says Camp, a life coach and author of *Start with No* (Crown Business, 2002), a primer on negotiating.

People who find decision-making difficult tend to lack that vision, Camp says. For those who fret about making up their minds, Camp offers advice on how to streamline the process.

Look at your long-term aim. Decisions are easier if you know where you're going. If you don't, "you stagnate on decisions," Camp says.

Keep a decisions journal. Each day, jot down an easy decision (what to wear to work, what to order for lunch) and note why it was easy. Internalizing the process of making small low-risk decisions helps make the big ones simpler.

It's okay to be wrong. "The most effective decision-makers aren't afraid to decide because they know they can correct a bad decision," Camp explains.

It's okay to change your mind. "That's admitting you messed up, and you can fix it."

Try not to overthink a decision. Turning your thoughts over and over is "a method of procrastination that comes with a lack of vision," Camp says. It isn't deciding, it's stalling.

Buy yourself time. If you're unable to decide something, give yourself a set number of days to do research or check on sources before you make a decision. "That's a plan of action; that's effective decision-making," Camp says.

Scarlett
rule 10

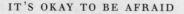

> ## IT'S OKAY TO BE AFRAID

*Her first terrified impulse was to hide in the closet, crawl under the
bed, fly down the back stairs and run screaming to the swamp. . . .*

—*Gone with the Wind*

Courage is being scared to death but saddling up anyway.

—John Wayne

Scarlett's legions of admirers love to think of her as fearless, a paragon of courage in the face of poverty, hunger,
and the unspeakable horrors of war. That's like thinking
Melanie really was a mealy-mouthed ninny or that Ashley
really, truly, and deeply loved Scarlett.

In fact, our heroine spent more than a little time quaking

in her hand-made Moroccan slippers. If Scarlett had allowed it to, fear could easily have governed her life.

Like any sensible person, Scarlett was terrified as the Civil War came to a head in Atlanta, with General William Tecumseh Sherman's troops encircling the city and the Confederate Army creating its own havoc, destroying the city's supplies and munitions to keep them out of Sherman's hands. Scarlett was scared witless when the Union Army paid calls on Tara and when Tara's former overseer threatened to take Tara from her.

What *Gone with the Wind* fan can forget Scarlett's recurring nightmare, the dream that woke her in a cold sweat, her heart pounding, her blood racing through her veins? She was lost in a fog, running and running. To where, she had no idea; she always woke up before the dream ended. The dream terrified her, sometimes more than her waking life did.

Scarlett felt afraid far more often than she felt brave. But she refused to let a racing heart or clammy hands stop her from taking action. That's the very definition of courage: acting in the face of abject fear. While hardly fearless, Scarlett O'Hara had courage in spades.

Fear is the phone ringing at three in the morning. It's those anxious days between the biopsy and the moment the doctor calls with the results. It's losing sight of a child, even for a split second. It's seeing a husband walk through the front door, shoulders slumped, not his usual glad-to-be-home self. Fear is definitely not what it's made out to be on *The Fear Factor*. Eating bugs and diving headfirst into a vat of leeches has nothing to do with fear, especially when the reward is a tidy sum of money.

Anyone who believes that *Don't be afraid* is sound, actionable advice needs a primer in human physiology. A normal human being can't refuse to be afraid, any more than she can refuse to be sad or happy. Fear is a useful emotion. Fear tells the mind and body that something is wrong and then prepares the body for action. Adrenaline flows to the muscles. The heart beats at two to three times its resting rate. The eyes dilate to improve vision. Blood stops flowing to the skin. The digestive system shuts down, as does the immune system. All the body's resources are ready to be devoted to the fight—or flight—at hand.

Scarlett knew this and did exactly the right thing. She acknowledged that she was afraid and then surfed to action on that fear, sometimes morphing it into anger, an even better catalyst for action. Scarlett knew that feeling fear isn't an issue, but letting fear take control is.

If you let fear dictate your life, you'll miss out on so much. You'll be afraid to ask for a raise or a promotion, thus hamstringing your career. If you really want to go back to school for that MBA or MFA but are afraid you're too old or have no time, you'll miss out on one of life's finest pleasures: a higher education. Fear of moving to a new city, buying a new home, or asking a would-be friend to meet you for coffee can rob you of new opportunities. Fear of high winding roads will keep you off some of the most beautiful highways in the country, among them the Pacific Coast Highway and Highways 89 and 29, which wind around Lake Tahoe.

The trick to harnessing fear is first to acknowledge that

you're afraid, as Scarlett did so many times. Second is to push on despite your fear, not cower in a corner, scared into inaction. How to do this?

Remember that nothing in life is totally safe. Not riding in your own car even with the seat belt on, not crossing the street in front of your house, not taking a bite of that delicious-looking filet mignon at your favorite steak house—not even walking, seeing that our body weight is balanced on two pieces of flesh each measuring roughly thirty square inches (a size 9 female foot, anyway). Literally every step you take in life carries risks—some minor, some major, but risks just the same.

Weigh those risks. If you're afraid to take an action because it might kill you—well, nobody's going to argue with you there. If an action terrifies you because you might lose money, that's probably a wise fear, too. If it's more money than you can afford to lose, congratulations; you let fear make a great decision for you. If you can afford to lose the money and the thrill is worth it, go ahead and take the plunge. Though anyone who's ever ridden a big-city subway might advise steering clear of those shell-game players, no matter how flush you're feeling. Just like the house always wins, so do those players, no matter how absolutely sure you are that the pea is under shell number one.

Try not to confuse fear with anxiety. "Fear" that your great new guy won't call again after that lovely first date is really anxiety, as are the jitters before a test or a job interview, or the way your hands sometimes shake while you open an envelope that might contain unpleasant—not bad—news.

Speaking of anxiety, here's one to master, and quickly: medical anxiety. Avoiding the doctor won't make the weird lump go away or the merciless headaches stop. The only way to assuage that particular anxiety (and fix what's ailing you) is to call the doctor, make an appointment, and go. Whatever happens, you'll handle it.

And you *can* handle it. If you think you're not equipped to handle life's future fears, look to your past and conjure up the worst thing that has ever happened to you. Don't dismiss how awful the experience was; congratulate yourself for surviving it and then put the experience in your fear-surviving toolbox.

If you're a normal person, you'll pull out that toolbox time and time again, because life is as full of fearful moments as it is of joyful or depressing ones. Go ahead, be afraid. As Scarlett so beautifully shows us, there's no shame in being afraid, only in being a coward.

Scarlett lesson

GETTING PAST FEAR

Much of Scarlett's ability to get past fear lay in her ability to act even when she was deathly afraid. How? "She was forced to do things, and when we're forced, we don't have a choice," says Susan Jeffers, author of *Feel the Fear and Do It Anyway* (Ballantine Books, 1988). Having no choice is such a powerful motivator that Jeffers feels "sorry for women and men who aren't forced to get out there and create a life for themselves."

She offers advice on how to conquer what can be a debilitating emotion.

Do what you're afraid to do. If you're afraid to fly, fly. If you're afraid to drive on the highway, drive on the highway. The first time is heart-stopping, "but after you do it for a while, you're comfortable," Jeffers says.

Expand your comfort zone. "Every day, do something you're afraid to do," Jeffers says. Ask your boss for extra vacation time, make a decision alone, make a phone call you've been putting off. "Little by little, your life gets bigger and bigger."

Collect heroes. Search history books, newspapers, and magazines for men and women whose courage you admire. Look to them as personal role models when you're faced with a scary situation.

Let go of the outcome. If you're avoiding an action out of fear of failure, tell yourself you don't care what happens. Give the speech, make the call; if it doesn't go perfectly, you'll do better next time. "Stop having expectations as to how everything will turn out," Jeffers says.

Practice affirmation. It might sound New Agey but Jeffers says it works. Say to yourself, *Whatever happens I'll handle it.* "That's such a powerful statement." Another affirmation Jeffers likes, no matter what's crashing and burning: *This is all happening perfectly.*

Scarlett rule 11

ROLL WITH THE CHANGES

There was no going back and she was going forward.

—*Gone with the Wind*

I want to be part of what is to come.

—Coco Chanel

Imagine a high school English class deconstructing *Gone with the Wind*. As the students work through the pages, pointing out foreshadowing and searching for the denouement, they'll discover several themes: survival; gumption (an old-fashioned, Southern-flavored word, and author Margaret Mitchell's favorite to describe the point of her novel); love and loss, one of literature's favorite subjects; and one more—coping with change.

Gone with the Wind spans twelve years, and during those

twelve years Scarlett O'Hara's circumstances changed several times—drastically. At sixteen, Scarlett was a carefree teenage girl. Barely three years later, she was a single mother scrambling to maintain a scrubby farm. Her mother was dead and her father, addled and vague, was probably suffering from Alzheimer's. Fast-forward two more years and Scarlett was married to her second husband, mother to a second child, and manager of two successful businesses. And by the end of the story, Scarlett was once again rich and secure. But she had suffered the unimaginable pain of losing a child, and her husband had deserted her. Most women don't see in a lifetime what Scarlett saw in those dozen years.

Scarlett coped with change the way a chameleon adapts to new surroundings: She altered her surface, morphing from a pampered Southern girl accustomed to nibbling at life from a silver platter into a no-nonsense businesswoman responsible for feeding not only herself but her extended family as well. The formerly deferential daughter treated her father, in his diminished state, as a child. Formerly always kind to slaves, as her mother had instructed her, Scarlett became nearly as hard-hearted as a plantation overseer. In an amazingly swift attitude adjustment, Scarlett adapted to the life of a farmer rather than a plantation owner's daughter.

Unlike Ashley and even Melanie, who remained fixed in the old South's gentle way of life, Scarlett adapted to her new life with an alacrity that makes one wonder how much she really changed. Did Scarlett's veneer, which grows thicker and tougher with the turn of each page, signal a true metamorphosis of her character?

I doubt it. Appearances and status of birth aside, Scarlett

was never a gentlewoman. Had history not intervened—had Scarlett become a plantation owner's wife—those particular velvet handcuffs would have chafed as surely as the pebbles on Tara's paths cut through her tattered shoes. The war and Reconstruction enabled Scarlett to become the woman she was born to be: a successful business owner, as much master of her own destiny as the late nineteenth century allowed her to be.

As capably as Scarlett dealt with change, she lacked the skills to perceive that others deal with change differently but also effectively. She failed to understand how Melanie and those like her could remain genteel and cling to vestiges of their old life when, to Scarlett, all that remained of it was the forlorn skeletons of ravaged plantations.

Scarlett didn't even attempt to understand that Melanie and the old guard, so like Ellen with their cotton-soft exteriors and spun-steel insides, were survivors just as assuredly as she was. In fact, they enjoyed an advantage that Scarlett did not. They had meshed the best of the old world with the best of the new, and, if not happy, they were content.

For Scarlett, a tough shell was the only weapon with which to battle change. She couldn't imagine that a core of tempered steel could do the same.

L ife hands out all sorts of changes. Sudden and gradual, societal and individual, minor and major. Which changes are easier to roll with? A thinking person might choose sudden, massive change, perhaps of a historical nature, over small, gradual changes, because so little is left to choice. Scarlett and her fellow Southerners, at least the ones who wished to remain alive, had no choice but to deal with the Civil War and its aftermath. These days, people for whom travel is part of their life must deal with the consequences of September 11, 2001. No more mad dashes for planes, no more complacent feelings of safety—not with the threat of terrorist attacks shadowing the entire world.

But there's much to be said for change that takes place gradually, bit by bit, over time. Any person over seventy will tell you that she's dealt with the major technological changes in her lifetime—cell phones, affordable air travel, automatic transmissions, the Internet, e-tickets, self-service checkout lanes—because they've entered her life slowly, one technological advancement at a time.

Yet some little-by-little changes seem more difficult to handle than sudden sweeping ones. Aging, for instance. Everyone expects to age (it certainly beats the alternative!), but most women are shocked by its realities. The winsome wrinkle-free girl you feel like on the inside meets a wrinkled gray-haired stranger when she looks into the mirror. Running three miles used to be a breeze, and then one day it's tough to jog even a mile. Late-night dancing and a wee-hours breakfast are exhilarating, and then, almost overnight, a 7 P.M. dinner and 10 P.M. bedtime feel as relaxing as a spa vacation.

The first way people can deal with change gracefully is to accept it as part of a normal, healthy life. Growing things change; dead things do not. Yes, it's comforting, and tempting, to rely on the past to direct the future: "We've always done it this way." But people who resist change turn into living dinosaurs and soon become fossils: cool to have on a shelf but not much use to anyone and not much fun, either. Who enjoys being around an old person who begins every sentence with "Back in my day . . ."?

The second way to adapt well to change is to consider the bright side. When successful adapters get a new boss at work, they're happy for their former boss, especially if she's left for a better opportunity, but they keep themselves open to the varied career and professional insights a new boss may bring to the table. Even if, after a few months, they reasonably and objectively reach the conclusion that the new boss stinks, they have still learned from her mistakes.

There's even a bright side to aging, most elegantly encapsulated in the saying *Youth is wasted on the young*. Think back to your twenties, the decade when women look their best and are most likely to engage in unwise and shortsighted actions. Tattoos and body piercings are minor follies; having an inappropriate affair or rushing into a bad marriage is a major mistake. I would bet that every woman over forty looks back to at least one move she made in her twenties with perhaps not regret but certainly with amazement: *How could I have been so dumb?* Most people as they get older become more circumspect, more forgiving, and more accepting of the world and the people who live in it.

The third way people successfully deal with change is to use the tools they have at hand. For some women, it's people: their husband, the friends they've had since grade school, or confidantes who might have gone through similar changes— moves, marriages, divorce, children, jobs lost and jobs gained.

For other women, it might be technology: a box of L'Oréal that's exactly the hair color they always dreamed of, regular Botox or Restylane injections, or even plastic surgery. Not too long ago, *Women's Wear Daily*, the bible of the fashion industry, quoted forty-something actress Julianne Moore on the subject of plastic surgery: "I think imperfections are important . . . you only get to be real by being imperfect." That's easy for the porcelain-skinned auburn-haired Ms. Moore to say; she was born practically perfect, and as a successful actress she possesses the resources to stay that way. For other women, a face-lift might be just the thing they need to live out the rest of their lives with confidence and happiness.

A sense of humor helps, too. That's the driving theory behind the Red Hat Society, a national group of women over fifty who meet for tea (a stereotypical old-lady activity) dressed in red hats and purple dresses. They're not just aging gracefully, they're calling attention to the whole affair. Even if you'd rather be like a Desperate Housewife and enter your sixth decade in low-rise jeans and a tight sweater, you've got to admire the Red Hat gals for their creativity, not to mention their public-relations savvy.

Scarlett's bull-by-the-horns approach to change left her little patience for those who approached it differently. Still, she refused to let the past govern her future and stepped neatly over her many hurdles. What's not to admire?

RELOCATING, THE PAINLESS WAY

Scarlett divided her time between Tara and her home in Atlanta, but she never suffered the pain of moving to a completely new place. Most Americans today relocate more than
once in a lifetime: Each year, anywhere from 16 to 21 percent
of the population packs up and moves.

It's difficult to leave a beloved familiar place and put down
roots elsewhere; it's sad, too. "Accept the fact that you're going
to mourn," says Leslie Levine, author of *Will This Place Ever
Feel like Home?: Simple Advice for Settling In After You Move*
(McGraw-Hill, 2002). Moving means losing a house, friends,
a sense of community, and sometimes proximity to family.
Levine, who moved three times in twenty years, says you can
even miss things you thought you hated, like a balky garage-
door opener or the grungy corner store.

To prepare yourself mentally for a move, avoid thinking in
terms of *never*, as in *I'll never make new friends* or *I'll never
find my way*. Instead, regard the move as a challenge and compare it with other challenges you've met successfully: transi-
tioning to a new job, helping your child through a crisis, even
a previous move. "You can draw on those strengths," Levine
says.

If you're a relocating spouse, check to see if your partner's
company offers any relocation assistance. Levine's home office

in Rochester, New York, had a built-in desk and shelves; when her husband's company moved them to Illinois, she asked for, and got, an allowance to buy new office furniture.

Once you arrive in your new surroundings, take charge of your social life. "It's not like the olden days; people won't come over with a plate of brownies," Levine says. "The onus falls on the person who moves." Get to know your new community. Visit the library, where the vestibule and bulletin boards hold a wealth of information on community goings-on. Volunteer, if you have time, and shop at locally owned stores to plug into and support the local economy.

Don't sabotage yourself by constantly talking about your former home and community, no matter how much you miss them. "Human nature is to think *She must not like it here, so I won't extend myself,*" Levine says.

Scarlett rule 12

THINK MORE LIKE A MAN

She knew what she wanted and she went after it by the shortest route, like a man.
                                        —Gone with the Wind

"Why can't a woman be more like a man?"
                —Professor Henry Higgins in Alan Jay Lerner's *My Fair Lady*

In business, in romance, in relationships, in navigating everyday life, Scarlett O'Hara rarely acted like the Southern belle she was brought up to be. Sure, she simpered and flirted when it suited her purposes. But when Scarlett wanted something, her girlish charm evaporated like morning mist on a hot Georgia day. She spoke her mind. She made decisions. She wasn't afraid to make money—quite a lot of it.

Beneath her feminine exterior, Scarlett harbored more than a few masculine qualities. Like Rhett and Ashley, she regarded the war as a lost cause, not a noble one. She pursued her career with unrelenting passion. She didn't want children, nor did she have patience with them.

Like Gordon Gekko of *Wall Street* fame, Scarlett built her successful businesses on shady business practices. Fortunately, the Old South's code of chivalry survived the war and prevented Scarlett's male competitors from revealing those business tactics to customers. Luckily for Scarlett, she had no female competitors.

L ike the salt that makes chocolate-chip cookies so good or the messy hairdo that sets off a formal evening gown to perfection, Scarlett's personality blended feminine and masculine with stunning results. So did Rhett's, for that matter. Nobody would mistake tall, dark, and muscular Rhett for anything but a man, and his choice of flowered waistcoats only enhanced his masculinity.

The most appealing people know, and use, the power of gender bending. Men love it when a woman reads the sports pages, drives a stick shift, or picks up the check. Women love it when a man holds the baby, cooks dinner, or takes them shopping for clothes. Such behavior is attractive to the opposite sex and makes life infinitely more interesting. No matter what your gender, it's fun to do things differently: to drive if most of the time you're the passenger; to cook if most times you order takeout; to read a map if you usually stop at a gas station for directions.

Here's when Scarlett let her masculine side show, and how you can follow suit.

Take the wheel.
When Rhett deserted Scarlett and her entourage as they fled Atlanta, Scarlett drove the tired horse and heavy wagon to Tara herself. *Suggestion:* If you always let your boyfriend or girlfriend drive, take the wheel for once. It's fun, and it lets your partner relax and hunt for out-of-state license plates.

Make a decision.
Scarlett never spent more than a few minutes making a decision; her quickness bewildered Frank Kennedy, who was accustomed to women who made decisions in a much more methodical fashion. *Suggestion:* If your habit is to mull each move you make for days, try making a snap decision.

Organize a play date.
As a child, Scarlett was a tomboy, and as an adult she enjoyed walking and horseback riding. *Suggestion:* If you usually meet friends for a beer or a glass of wine, try gathering instead at a park for a game of Frisbee or softball.

Clean your plate.
Scarlett was annoyed when Mammy made her stuff herself before the barbecue; she wasn't ashamed of her hearty appetite. *Suggestion:* If you really want to finish that pasta carbonara, don't worry what your date will think. Finish it, and then order some tiramisu.

Mow the lawn.

When Scarlett found herself one of the few able-bodied people at Tara, she didn't balk at gardening—or any other tough work, for that matter. She did what needed to be done. *Suggestion:* Swap chores. If you usually cook, do the yard work. If you're on cleanup duty, cook. If you never take out the garbage, take out the garbage.

Get dressed fast.

Even vain Scarlett could leave the house with nothing more than a comb run through her hair and a quick pinch of her cheeks (rouge, for nice girls). *Suggestion:* Develop a five-minute version of your usual toilette. Life's too short to spend hours in the bathroom.

Scarlett wasn't afraid to be a woman; nor was she afraid to be a man when the situation called for it. The yin-yang combo worked wonders for her. Try it and see what it does for you.

NEGOTIATE LIKE A PRO

Atlanta viewed Scarlett's trading skills as unpleasantly unfeminine. More than a century later, negotiating is still seen as a man's game, one that women either can't or won't play. Nonsense, says Leslie Whitaker, author, along with Elizabeth

Austin, of *The Good Girl's Guide to Negotiating* (Little, Brown, 2001). Women possess the same negotiating skills as men and may even have a leg up, thanks to their natural empathy and listening skills. Here's how to negotiate like a pro, no matter which chromosomes you have.

Do your research. Find out how much the owners paid for the house you want to buy, or check the price of that car on edmunds.com or with another car buyers' resource. Information is power at the bargaining table.

Be assertive. "Women confuse assertion with aggression, and that makes them afraid to ask for what they want," Whitaker says. Ask for what you want, and the battle is half over.

Be empathetic, not sympathetic. Sympathy makes you feel bad for the party at the other side of the table; empathy enables you to put yourself in their shoes. Sympathy will make you feel sorry for your company when you're asking for a big fat raise, while empathy will help you realize what a bargain they're getting with you: a top-notch, superproductive employee.

Learn when to be silent. Quiet stretches are key negotiating tools, Whitaker says. If you hear an offer you don't like, don't say anything. Let the other side jump in with a better one.

Practice the art of waiting. Don't always take the initiative in negotiations; wait for the other side to make the first offer and then get the ball rolling. At your next job interview, for instance, don't reveal how much you'd like to make. Instead, wait until your prospective employer gives you a salary range and take it from there.

Be prepared to be slightly unhappy. Negotiations are a give-and-take situation; you might end up with most of what you want but not everything. As long as the deal meets your priorities, you can leave the table satisfied.

Scarlett
rule 13

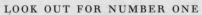

LOOK OUT FOR NUMBER ONE

She must not count on anything or anybody but herself.

—*Gone with the Wind*

Take life in your own hands and what happens? A terrible thing: no one to blame.

—Erica Jong

Katie Scarlett O'Hara's social status nearly guaranteed she'd never have to take care of herself. Either Mammy or one of Tara's other ninety-nine slaves would make sure the mistress of the manor didn't have to lift a finger unless it was absolutely necessary. They'd dress her, bathe her, serve her breakfast in bed, soothe her when she was upset, and pretend to share in her joyous moments. What they couldn't handle, her parents would. And when marriage moved Scarlett from their household into her husband's, his slaves would take over where hers left off.

The war changed all that, robbing Scarlett of her luxurious life and handing her widowhood and motherhood, two titles she was unprepared for and unwilling to accept. Still, Scarlett quickly turned from a coddled girl into a self-reliant woman. One minute she was pushing away the ham and hotcakes Mammy commanded her to eat before the barbecue; the next she was scraping meals together from peanuts, yams, and other Southern staples the Yankees hadn't known enough to steal. One minute she was deciding which gown to wear; practically the next, she was making life-and-death decisions for her family.

All the while, Scarlett was learning to rely on herself and herself only: working overtime at the mills, feverishly stockpiling money. Taking charge of her life, she accepted responsibility for every outcome, failures as well as successes.

Watching Scarlett jump over whatever hurdles stood in her way, the impulse is to cheer her on: "Run, Scarlett, run!" The only problem is that Scarlett, like Forrest Gump, sometimes didn't know when to stop.

It's unsettling to hear a person characterized as "looking out for number one." Is it a compliment, praising this person for her self-reliance and entrepreneurship? Or is it an insult, slamming her for being a selfish opportunist?

It should be a compliment. Looking out for number one makes sense, especially for the busy woman who cares for her kids, her partner, her parents, and then finally herself, if she has any spare time or energy left. No wonder women's magazines and newspapers run so many stories on how to overcome fatigue. Exhaustion among women seems almost epidemic.

Perhaps redirecting a little time and energy into self-care and self-preservation would turn the tide. Not only is it satisfying to put yourself first; it's critical to survival. Flight attendants remind us to put on our oxygen masks before helping others; mother bears feed themselves before they feed their cubs. Flight attendants and wild bears know what you should know: Making yourself a priority is not selfish, nor will it diminish your capacity as a boss, wife, mother, daughter, or friend.

Begin with your health. Scarlett describes her mother, Ellen, as forgoing food and rest for the sake of her household. Such selfless devotion weakened her so mightily that Ellen succumbed to typhoid fever; when her family needed her most, she was resting peacefully in Tara's graveyard. Contemporary women seem to be following Ellen's lead. Research released in 2005 by the National Women's Health Resource Center showed that while 44 percent of women value having a healthy family, only 15 percent place a premium on eating healthfully themselves.

The overriding reason these women cited for putting their families first and themselves last: lack of time. But let's use a day's worth of meals to put "lack of time" into perspective. For more than a few women, a daily meal plan looks like this: coffee for breakfast, fast food or nothing for lunch, chips or processed cheese crackers from a vending machine for a midday snack, and then dinner, when it's time to cram the entire day's nutritional needs into one famished sitting.

But really, how long does it take to grab a bowl of cereal, a banana, or a piece of toast while the kids are having their breakfast or while you're listening to the traffic and weather reports? And how difficult or time-consuming is it to throw a Lean Cuisine and an apple into a thermal bag for lunch? Even Scarlett, ever mindful of preserving her tiny waist, enjoyed her meals. When she and Rhett honeymooned in New Orleans, Scarlett stuffed herself with seafood and cream puffs, the better to forget the hunger years at Tara.

Make time for meals, for sleep, and for exercise, too, even if it's a fifteen-minute walk with the dog in the morning. More and more, researchers are discovering that exercise is a tonic for your mind as well as your body. Regular exercise can stave off depression, and there's nothing like it for working out a thorny problem. Don't feel you have to run at an eight-minute-mile pace; a brisk walk will do. Or try swimming for a refreshing half hour or so. Perhaps because it renders the body weightless, swimming has the magical ability, at least temporarily, to solve all of life's problems.

It seems such selfish business, this looking out for number one. But consider this: If you owned a business, would you hire a crabby, tired, hungry person to work for you? Probably not. Exhausted people don't make good workers—or mothers, spouses, or friends, for that matter. The next time a friend tells you to take care, listen. Scarlett did.

HAPPY BIRTHDAY TO YOU!

I'd bet Scarlett was a Leo, but I have no way of knowing for sure. *Gone with the Wind* never mentions the date of Scarlett's birth or any celebrations of it. Perhaps Margaret Mitchell didn't enjoy her own birthday—if so, she wouldn't be alone.

Women detest birthdays because the passing of one more year almost assuredly turns up one more gray hair, another wrinkle, a few more sags in a once-firm figure. But isn't having a birthday so much better than the alternative?

Don't ignore your next birthday. Celebrate it as the life-affirming event it is. You don't need cupcakes or a game of Pin the Tail on the Donkey to celebrate. Invite a few friends over for wine and hors d'oeuvres and don't fuss if they bring gifts. Unwrapping a gift—struggling with a stubborn ribbon, hearing the crackle of paper, wondering what on earth is inside—is one of life's great pleasures.

If it's a decade-marking birthday, take yourself to dinner. It doesn't have to be a fancy place; your favorite ethnic dive will do nicely. If your parents are alive, write them a thank-you note, especially your mom; she did all the heavy lifting on your actual birth day.

And here's a totally shameless me-first move: If your

family is the gift-giving type, present them with a good old-fashioned birthday list to let them know exactly what you want. *Oh, no,* you might protest, *that's just too self-centered, too calculating.* Perhaps it is. But on your birthday, of all days, don't you deserve it?

Scarlett
rule 14

> GROW UP

"I think you are still a child." —Rhett to Scarlett, *Gone with the Wind*

How old would you be if you didn't know how old you were?

—Satchel Paige, legendary pitcher and
member of the Baseball Hall of Fame

It is a truth universally acknowledged that today's teenage girls should be in high school, studying history and geometry and Spanish and just starting to develop the social skills that will lead to love and perhaps marriage.

Not in Scarlett's day. In the antebellum South, teenage girls born into society's top tier would complete a few years of finishing school and then get right down to the serious work of finding a husband and starting a family. Scarlett married Charles Hamilton when she was sixteen, considered back then to be just about the right age for marriage.

Scarlett occupied the social stratum of an adult, may have been a fledgling adult chronologically, and by her own vain assessment had a woman's figure. Every once in a while, Scarlett even acted like an adult, as when she took on the burden of caring for her extended family after returning to Tara to find it nearly ruined.

But in so many ways, Scarlett remained a girl. She nursed her crush on Ashley long after she should have let it pass. She pouted when she didn't get her way. She bullied her sisters, and she refused to take no for an answer. She failed to see the effect of her actions on others' lives; she was as self-centered as a child. Most children grow out of that me-first stage. Scarlett never did.

O*h, grow up!* is one of our time's most withering insults. Thoughtless words and actions earn an *Oh, grow up!* The phrase knocks the intended receiver out of the realm of cherished adulthood and back to the land of blankies, sippy cups, and forced naps, territory few thinking adults would willingly reoccupy.

Earth is populated with plenty of fine non-grown-ups. England's Prince Harry acted like a non-grown-up when he paraded around in that swastika on Halloween. Only a child could be that shallow, wearing, for the fun of it, an emblem that cost 700,000 British soldiers their lives. Runaway bride

Jennifer Wilbanks, another non-adult, chose not only to run from her problems but to stage a kidnapping scam that scapegoated Hispanic Americans.

Children who survive a major falling-out with their parents take a giant step forward on the path to adulthood. Most people love their parents and, out of love, take all sorts of drastic measures to shield them. They smoke, but not in their parents' presence; they pretend they're not living with someone when they are. Perhaps that's why Scarlett never grew up. Since her mother was dead and her father senile, she never had to present them with the person she had become and risk their disapproval. Showing your real self to your parents, no matter how loudly you know they'll squall, requires a steely inner core of maturity that can take a lifetime to amass.

Being a grown-up also requires a measure of self-sufficiency. If you're an adult, you should live on your own. Of course there's no shame in living with your parents; more and more kids saddled with post-college debt find themselves back in their old bedrooms after graduation. The shame is in letting your mom do your laundry and tidy up your room or in neglecting to pay even nominal rent. By the same token, having your own place is no badge of adulthood—that is, if you take sacks of laundry home on weekends, consistently show up for visits right around dinnertime, present your parents with the puppy your lease expressly forbids, unfailingly hit them up for a loan every time you see them, borrow their car without asking . . . you get the picture. It's not *where* you live, but *how* that makes you either an adult or an overgrown teenager.

Here's a brief checklist of how grown-ups live.

* They keep their promises.
* They show up on time.
* They're where they say they are.
* They accept no for an answer when no is the answer.
* They learn to work with people and not constantly do battle with the world.
* They listen to others.
* They willingly cede the spotlight to others at a party, at the office, or in other social situations.
* They recognize that they're part of a larger community.
* They accept that they are mortal beings and look out for their own safety accordingly.
* They know it's human to have emotions, and as adult human beings they control these emotions.

Scarlett's successes as an adult woman, so often compromised by her childish self, create the intrigue that makes *Gone with the Wind* such a compelling tale. But while that blend is entrancing in literature, it rarely works in real life. Don't be a Scarlett. Grow up.

BRAT, BE GONE!

Sulking and sobbing aren't exactly mature behaviors, but grown-ups indulge in them every day, says Pauline Wallin, a Pennsylvania-based psychologist and author of *Tame Your Inner Brat* (Beyond Words Publishing, 2001). And it gets worse: Overeating, overspending, overdrinking, and other indulgences are sure signs that your inner brat's taken the wheel. "If you regret it later, then it's your inner brat," Wallin says, and she explains how to send your "inner brat" back to her room.

Anticipate the brat's arrival. You'll feel it start to emerge when you feel underappreciated or when your expectations, even if you haven't voiced them, haven't been met. "Women expect people to read their minds," Wallin says.

Calm down. Your inner brat is raw emotion, hell-bent on filling a particular need. "Get in touch with the rational part of yourself," Wallin says. One tip: Try to discern whether people around you are reacting the same way to a situation or if it's only you. If it's only you, the brat is suspect.

Put your adult self in charge. You wouldn't argue with a four-year-old about a cookie, so don't argue with your inner brat.

Let your adult self decide what to do and then proceed with that action, ignoring the whining coming from inside.

Be consistent and persistent. Once you decide to ignore your inner brat's desire to rant or rave, overspend or overeat, ignore that urge consistently. Again, think of children. As Wallin suggests, "If you're not consistent and persistent with children, they keep at it."

Try a little perspective. A rude clerk, a bad driver, a snagged stocking: Will it matter in a week, a day, or even an hour? Placing a small annoyance in the grand scheme of life works wonders in taming your inner brat, Wallin says.

Scarlett
rule 15

FIND YOUR NICHE

She was Gerald's own daughter and the shrewd trading instinct she had inherited was now sharpened by her needs.

—*Gone with the Wind*

Success is not the key to happiness. Happiness is the key to success. If you love what you are doing, you will be successful.

—Albert Schweitzer

Olivia de Havilland, who played Melanie Hamilton in *Gone with the Wind*, said it best: "Scarlett was a career girl." Miss de Havilland is right. Had Scarlett been born in the latter half of the twentieth century instead of in the middle of the nineteenth, she'd wear Armani suits, carry a Coach brief-case, and occupy a corner office before she turned thirty.

Scarlett's parents would have recognized her flair for business early on, in the way she decided what she wanted and then employed every resource at her disposal to get it. They would have spotted leadership skills in her fearless tree climbing and daredevil horseback riding. A twentieth-century Gerald would have urged Scarlett to get an MBA first and worry about the MRS after she made senior VP.

Timing is everything, though, and fate dropped Scarlett into an era that placed a premium on a woman's beauty and gentle manners but no value on her ability to think. Women were allowed to use their brains only as long they hid the process from men, and smart women mastered that ability. Book-loving women who enjoyed a brisk literary discussion as much as a brisk reel were dismissed as bluestockings, equivalent to the modern egghead or nerd.

Society also offered women few options. The top social sphere of the Old South presented only one lifestyle: Marry, raise a family, run the plantation. Boys were encouraged to take on the family business, but if they wanted they could go to college and on a European grand tour before settling down to work. Most girls had no opportunity to learn or travel. Their classroom was their front parlor, where they were taught to read and write, embroider, sing, play piano, sit and stand and walk gracefully, and dance, all in the hopes of someday luring a suitable husband to their side. Some girls went to finishing school, but the experience was more social than educational. Even if they didn't marry, these girls had so much family money that they didn't have to earn a living.

The rules defining gender roles bent a little after the war. Women were still expected to defer to men and raise babies and put their brains more or less in cold storage. But women, especially widows, were finally allowed to earn a living. Such opportunities might turn the most unusual candidates into take-charge entrepreneurs; Mrs. Merriwether, the humorless matron, parlayed her pie-making skills into a prosperous bakery.

And Scarlett O'Hara, the toast of Clayton County, turned into a sharp businesswoman, relishing the challenges of running the store and the mill and happily leaving her children in Melanie's care. Scarlett's take-no-prisoners personality was so suited to bustling Atlanta's postwar economy that it's difficult to imagine her as happy in any other kind of life.

Scarlett played two major roles in her life: pampered plantation owner's daughter and take-charge businesswoman. Born into the first lifestyle and forced into the second, Scarlett didn't find those niches as much as they found her. So many women stumble into their life's work or situation. They marry their high school sweetheart right after graduation, begin a family, and end up a full-time mom. Or they find a job that pays the rent, stick with it, climb their company ladder, and end up a C-level executive.

There's so much to expect out of a job: a salary big enough to cover the bills, good benefits, colleagues congenial enough to be work friends if not weekend ones, a workplace reasonably close to home. Should you expect work to make you happy, too? I'd say yes. Over the course of a lifetime, people spend more time at work than they do at home, and more time with their co-workers than they do with their families.

The next time you're asked what you do for a living, step outside yourself and observe your reaction. Do your eyes light up? Do you grow animated, talking about your company, your colleagues, and your business trips? Or do you sigh, offer some vague description of your job, and then add, with another sigh, "It pays the rent"?

If talking about your job makes you wish fervently that you were having a conversation about a different subject, maybe it's time for a change. Life is too short to remain unenthusiastic. True, nobody will lie on a deathbed wishing they'd spent more time at the office, but plenty of people might wish they'd taken the time to find a more fulfilling career, one that dovetailed with their natural abilities or filled a need they had to make the world a better place.

It's not impossible to find a new niche, no matter how entrenched you are in your current groove. The first step is recognizing that you could be happier. Maybe you feel depressed some days for no reason. Maybe it's getting tougher and tougher to get to the office on time. Maybe your partner has pointed out that you're complaining about your job more than you usually do. Maybe your partner has even suggested that you investigate a new line of work.

The second step is to discover what you'd like to do. The Internet offers a wealth of aptitude tests, many of which are free just for registering. The site www.viastrengths.com capitalizes on the new theory that it's easier for us to work with our strengths rather than against our weaknesses. Princeton Review, the company that prepares millions of students for college board tests, offers a short free career quiz on its website (princetonreview.com). See assessment.com for a more detailed test called the Motivational Appraisal of Personal Potential. HumanMetrics.com offers a version of the famous Myers-Briggs Type Indicator. A few visits with a career coach might also help you point yourself in a different direction. The Association of Career Professionals signs its career-coach members to ethical standards; visit its website (www.acpinter national.org) for more information on coaching or to locate a coach in your city.

If the thought of a career coach or assessment test makes you uncomfortable, poll your friends and family for advice. Close friends and family members often notice skills that you either dismiss as unimportant or don't realize you possess, so ask your sister or best friend what she thinks you do best. Is it finding solutions to problems? Decorating a room? Fixing anything that's broken? Pay close attention for a few months and take note every time someone says *You're so good at [whatever]*. Or, if you already know which skills you have but aren't putting them to profitable use, listen to yourself. That's what Amy Scherber of New York's Amy's Bread did. Scherber, who trained to be a marketing executive, realized she loved baking. So she retrained at the Culinary Institute of America and worked as a pastry chef before opening her first bakery in 1992. Since then, her love of baking has grown into a hundred-employee business that supplies hundreds of New York restaurants and stores with delicious baked goods.

Your third step is to figure out how to put your talents to work. Not everyone can quit a job to pursue her dream. Health insurance (no small matter in a country with forty million uninsured citizens), a regular paycheck, and a dependable routine are all superb reasons to keep your day job. If your boss is interested in your happiness, share your dreams with her. Perhaps she can help you move to a new department that will allow you to use your innate skills, or perhaps she can add a few responsibilities (with a raise, of course) to your current job. Don't dismiss the idea out of hand—you never know until you ask.

If time permits, make your passion part of your life in another way. If you like to bake but don't have the resources to open a bakery or attend culinary school, bake fabulous birthday cakes for friends. If you like to repair things, fix your household's broken appliances. If you like to decorate, do up your own home in a way that elicits sighs of delight from visitors. Have some spare time? Volunteer for a cause that puts your passion to work. Care for sick people, help out at an animal shelter, work on the election campaign for a politician you respect. Paid work isn't the only outlet for passion. As Oscar Wilde remarked, "I put all my genius into my life; I put only my talent into my works."

Never think it's too late to find your passion. Until he was nearly sixty years old, Ray Kroc sold milk shake machines for a living. But he never stopped looking for his passion, and that's how he decided he could turn Dick and Mac McDonald's drive-through into the biggest restaurant company in the world. Madonna has a genius for finding her passion over and over again: Every few years, the singer discovers a new persona (punk, Marilyn Monroe–style glamour girl, boy toy, et cetera) that keeps her in the public eye and makes her millions of dollars. Brooke Shields also has a skill for finding passions; the child model morphed into a successful Broadway actress and, most recently, into a successful author with the publication of *Down Came the Rain*, a book chronicling her postpartum depression.

Finally, realize that losing your job or an equally dire situation might prove an opportunity for you to change to a career that's more comfortable and even more profitable. Adversity certainly pushed Scarlett into her career as a thriving businesswoman. Allow it—and other life changes—to do the same for you.

Scarlett
lesson

LOSE YOUR BIG "BUT"

Once Scarlett discovered business as her calling in life, she didn't thwart her future with doubts: *But what if I fail? But what if my friends are disappointed in me? But what if I succeed?* In her work as a Los Angeles–based life coach, T. C. Conroy helps clients with the hard work of overcoming the "buts" that stand in the way of their dreams. Here's what she suggests.

✦ Figure out what's stopping you from moving on. Putting others' needs first, being afraid to hurt feelings, or an overly broad sense of responsibility—fear that everything will fall apart if you're not in the picture—are common stumbling blocks to dreams, Conroy says.

✦ Take charge of your life. Conroy knows clients are ready for action when they say, "I'm tired of cruising along and taking what comes my way; I'm ready to create my reality."

✦ Stop saying you have no time for your dream. "If you met a hot guy, you'd free up some time," Conroy says pointedly.

✦ Ask for help. Your friends and family want you to succeed, so rely on them for support.

✦ If you can't do your dream big, do it small. Want to be a singer? Take voice lessons and volunteer to sing at a friend's wedding, or join a choir. If fashion's your thing, design clothes for friends or help them revamp their wardrobes. Start an e-commerce website if you've always dreamed of owning a store.

✦ If you can't seem to shake your fears, peer into your future. When her clients remain stuck, Conroy will say, "What does it look like for you three years from now, five years from now, when you're talking to your kids about their dreams and you didn't honor yours?" If that doesn't work, she'll take them "straight to their deathbed, as grim as that sounds." As she explains, "When you create that awareness, you'll find the courage to do what you need to do, or at least give it a shot."

Scarlett
rule 16

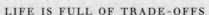

LIFE IS FULL OF TRADE-OFFS

"But there's a penalty attached, as there is to most things you want. It's loneliness."   —Rhett to Scarlett, *Gone with the Wind*

One half of knowing what you want is knowing what you must give up before you get it.
                    —Sidney Howard, writer of the *Gone with the Wind* screenplay

Scarlett O'Hara was street-smart and industrious. She was also competitive, adventurous, and resourceful. But she wasn't introspective.

As she single-mindedly chased her goal of never being hungry again, Scarlett never stopped to consider that every step she took on that path toward wealth and security required a trade-off, some sort of sacrifice. Scarlett traded a good relationship with her children for life as a shopkeeper and mill owner. She left her dream of being a great lady by the wayside in order to become a shrewd (and unscrupulous) trader. She gave up old family friends in favor of entertaining Yankee politicians at her glamorous mansion.

Those trade-offs, Scarlett figured, wouldn't be permanent. When she had money and time, she'd play with her children, be a great lady, entertain the right people, and repair the old family ties her reckless actions had destroyed.

She was wrong. Only after Scarlett was all but expelled from Atlanta society, after her children Wade and Ella had become afraid of her, and after her dreams of becoming a great lady had evaporated did she discover that time and money couldn't help her reverse her steps. Children can be nurtured and played with only for a short time. Friends can bear only so much disloyalty before they turn their backs for good. Kind, gentle people are always kind and gentle, rich or poor. Scarlett deluded herself into thinking that the choices she made were temporary, when in fact many of them were painfully permanent.

Everyday life involves hundreds of choices, ranging from the simple to the complicated and from the inconsequential to the monumental. Pasta or Chinese for dinner? California or Florida for vacation? A home in the city or in the suburbs? Employment at a traditional company or a work-from-home lifestyle? Simple everyday choices are hardly worth mulling over. If you don't have Chinese tonight, you can have it tomorrow; barring some catastrophe along the San Andreas Fault,

California will still be around if you choose to visit Disney-land this year.

The bigger choices are crucial; the rest of your life hinges on them. As important as making those decisions is realizing what you will give up once you choose a particular path. And you *will* give up something. Every choice, even a happy no-doubt-about-it decision that fulfills a lifelong dream, entails a sacrifice. Earning a living outside the structure of a corporation is immensely gratifying, but those who decide to work outside that structure sacrifice pensions and benefits, not to mention watercooler camaraderie. Even marriage, for all its glories, carries a few sacrifices. When you link your life forever with someone else's, you lose some freedom, and you sacrifice the possibility that there's someone out there who's an even better match for you.

Happy people weigh the consequences of big choices. They try to understand, as best as they can, what they stand to gain and lose with each decision. As a result, they're seldom sur-prised. New parents who fully apprehend the all-consuming responsibilities of parenthood don't complain (well, at least not that much) about suddenly being sleepless and 200 percent in the service of their new family member. Corporate employ-ees turned sole proprietors don't bemoan the fact that they have to wade through reams of paperwork to get health insur-ance; they realize that they've sacrificed the relative ease of group coverage by going solo.

People who understand the concept of sacrifice are much more confident about their life decisions. They don't envy those who have made the opposite choice. A mom who's confi-dent that her outside job is best, for her and her children, can say "to each her own" to her stay-at-home neighbor and vice versa. At the risk of ruffling some feathers, I will guess that a lack of confidence lies at the heart of the endless (and media-fueled) "mommy wars" between women who choose to stay home with their kids and women who choose to keep working. Can't we all trust one another, and ourselves, to decide what's best? Aren't there more important things to worry about than whose kids are in day care and whose aren't?

There's one way to enjoy the happiness and confidence of a well-made decision: Before you commit one way or another, research your options. Before quitting your job to become an independent contractor, talk to friends or former colleagues who have done this and find out what it's like to structure your day without a boss looking over your shoulder, to chase outstanding invoices, to create your own pension plan, and to ensure steady work. You might not like what you hear but choose to make the leap anyway; at least you'll know what to expect.

While Scarlett knew what to expect from the paths she chose, she had no idea of what the personal consequences would be. She bet that hard work and perseverance would gain her wealth and security; she did not bet that hard work would cost her a loving relationship with her children, the loyalty of her friends, and a precious link to her past. Scarlett is a positive role model in so many ways; who wouldn't want to have her resourcefulness, her zest for life? But in this case don't do as Scarlett did. Don't coast through life unaware of the consequences of your choices. Think a little. Reflect. Hindsight may be twenty-twenty, but foresight is even better.

AT WORK, YOU CAN HAVE IT ALL

Moms devoted to their jobs expect a bit of a trade-off. Obviously, time spent at the office is time not spent with their children. But working mothers who expect and settle for less pay should do a little research. Plenty of jobs pay women more than men and don't require a 24/7 commitment, either.

Warren Farrell, a political scientist and author of *Why Men Earn More: The Startling Truth Behind the Pay Gap—and What Women Can Do About It* (AMACOM, 2005), has identified twenty-five reasons why men make more than women. Among them: Women tend to choose jobs that are safe, with sane hours, and reasonable commutes, and with little pressure to travel or relocate. Because such jobs are desirable, "supply goes up, demand goes down, and pay goes down," Farrell explains.

But women can have it both ways: a safe and sane job that pays well. Farrell has found eighty professional fields that pay women more than men; overall, the more male-dominated a field, the better that field will pay women. Here are six of these professions and how much more they pay women over men.

+ Statistician: 135 percent more
+ Speech/language pathologist: 129 percent more
+ Financial analyst: 118 percent more

+ Radiation therapist: 111 percent more
+ Library worker: 110 percent more
+ Advertising/promotions manager: 105 percent more

Farrell has some advice for career-oriented women who plan to have children: Find a partner who's willing to stay home with the kids once they arrive. Assuming that the woman should always stay home "is the biggest deficiency in the culture at this time," Farrell says.

$\mathcal{S}$carlett
rule 17

APPEARANCES ARE DECEIVING

"Strange how these illusions will persist even in women as hard headed as you are."
—Rhett to Scarlett, *Gone with the Wind*

Keep your eyes wide open before marriage, half shut afterwards.
—Benjamin Franklin

Time after time I've wanted to reach into the pages of *Gone with the Wind*, grab Scarlett by the shoulders, and give her a good shake. How could one of literature's most pragmatic women hold on so tightly to so many fanciful notions?

Ashley, her first crush, gentility personified—of course he loved her! But he did not; he simply lusted after her. Melanie, so soft, so shy, so meek—of course she was a mealy-mouthed ninny. Wrong: Melanie was strong, loyal, and one of Scarlett's staunchest supporters. Rhett, the dark stranger banished from his own hometown, the daring blockade runner, he of the impudent tongue and brutally honest observations—of course he simply lusted after her! Wrong again: Rhett loved Scarlett from the start.

What is so amazing is not that Scarlett harbored illusions but that she nurtured them for so long. Time and again, evidence capable of shattering her false beliefs practically slapped her in the face. Ashley married Melanie and had a son with her. Melanie stuck by Scarlett despite Scarlett's transparent contempt for her. Rhett continued to love Scarlett even as Scarlett continued to moon after Ashley. Strong clues? Yes, and Scarlett ignored them all.

Melanie had to die for Scarlett to see her as the strong, noble woman she was. Ashley's flirtation with insanity, absently playing with Melanie's gloves as she lay dying in the next room, opened Scarlett's eyes to his many faults. Rhett had to waltz out the front door before Scarlett realized how deeply he loved her and how like him she was. Her illusions melted only after catastrophic events, events that occurred far too late to do her any good.

Sometimes it seems as if the earth—or at least the earth's celebrity news divisions—spins on make-believe. Celebrities live and die by illusion; fans thrive on the just-perfect version of a star's life and then recoil in horror when something goes wrong. Consider Brad Pitt and Jennifer Aniston: How could they be more perfect? Gorgeous, talented, rich—many people would sell their souls to Donald Trump for a fraction of Brad and Jen's perfection. But who knows what a lovely exterior shields? Perhaps their marriage skidded south the minute the honeymoon ended; maybe, for their careers' sake, they stayed together longer than they wanted to. At any rate, the public bought their illusion of perfection and, when that illusion cracked, bought *People* magazine to find out what went wrong, when in all likelihood it was nothing out of the ordinary. They were married. Married people have problems, and sometimes they get divorced. It happens all the time.

Illusions, whether they focus on celebrities or the hot single plumber next door, are fun, at least for a while. Who hasn't gone on a great first date and then gone to sleep fantasizing about walking down the aisle with this perfect human being? Maybe the fantasy lasts through the second date, or perhaps it stretches out for an entire month. But one evening the illusion shatters beyond repair. Mr. Perfect picks his teeth in public. Ms. Perfect tugs on her underwear while strolling down the street. Sometimes illusions melt so fast it's hard to keep from bursting into laughter. You can't wait to get home and tell your best friend all about it.

Sometimes illusions are necessary. Who could stay married for more than a few days without harboring at least some vague belief that their spouse is the most beautiful, kind, generous, and loving person in the universe? Those illusions help marriages survive the unbeautiful, unkind, ungenerous, and unloving realities of real life with another human being: crusty dishes scattered around the house, selfish possession of the remote control, stockings hanging on the shower rod, the

Sunday paper folded into origami, churlish arguments about whose turn it is to walk the dog. Nobody's perfect, but illusions help us believe otherwise.

Still, illusions can be dangerous. Without Scarlett's notions, there would be no *Gone with the Wind:* Her illusions were crucial to her personality and to the novel's plot. Yet what serves as a plot mover in a work of fiction can derail a real life. People want perfect marriages, careers, and family relationships so desperately that they allow illusions to survive long after their expiration date. The abusive husband? He'll change. The boss who keeps passing you over for promotion? One day she'll see you as the talented employee you are. The sister who calls only when she needs money? Any day now she'll invite you over for dinner and a movie, no strings attached.

What, then, can a thinking person do to keep illusions where they belong: a flavorful side dish on life's buffet but not the main course? The grade-school rhyme—"Stop, look, and listen before you cross the street; use your eyes, use your ears, and then use your feet"—springs to mind. What useful advice for all of life's journeys!

Stop.

Try not to be wowed by outward appearance, be it possessions, apparel, or physical attributes. Consider possessions. In this day and age, when Americans' debt far outweighs their savings, there's no way of telling whether that new car belongs to your neighbor or to the bank. There's no way to know how far in debt your guy went to fill his closet with John Varvatos suits or stock his apartment with mint-condition mid-century furniture. (On second thought, you may figure it out the tenth time he sticks you with the dinner check.) Nor do clothes always indicate a person's true fashion sense. Remember Bridget Jones thinking that Mark Darcy was a dorky reindeer-sweater type, when the sweater was a gift from Darcy's mother and he wore it to make her happy? And while society places such a premium on being "hot," looks don't mean a thing. Every person who's ever dated has a story about the hottie who turned out to be a jerk.

Look.

Does someone or something seem perfect? Look again, more closely, and you'll spot the imperfections. Seventeenth-century Dutch artists painted pictures of lovely blooming flowers, each leaf and petal wrought in glorious detail. But next to that delightful array, they'd paint a fly or a bug—some earthly element to tell the viewer that nothing's perfect. Bugs, as well as blossoms, are part of earth's bounty. It's not nice to seek actively for flaws in others; nobody wants to be that critical. But if you want to keep at least one foot in reality, remember that every person and every situation is flawed. Note at least one and keep it in your back pocket, not for ammunition but just as a reality check.

Listen.

Actions may speak louder than words, but words can be deafening. Many women learn the hard way that when a man tells her "I'm not cut out for marriage," "I'm bad at relationships," or "I never want kids," he is probably telling the truth. Trust people to know themselves, especially if they take the time and trouble to communicate a particular bit of self-knowledge to you.

Scarlett's path from illusion to enlightenment is one that so many women take. It's a road peppered with clues so obvious that we keep right on walking, and so many chances to trade illusion for reality that there's bound to be another just up the street. But for Scarlett, there wasn't. *Don't judge a book by its cover*, the saying goes. The sadder but wiser Scarlett would agree.

QUIT YOUR LOVE ADDICTION

Scarlett didn't only harbor dangerous illusions about Ashley, she was addicted to him, too. "In the beginning, it was just a schoolgirl crush," says Tina Tessina, a licensed psychotherapist in Long Beach, California, and author of *The Unofficial Guide to Dating Again* (John Wiley Publishing, 1998). But as Scarlett grew older, her fixation with Ashley interfered with her life—and that's the definition of an addiction, Tessina says. "Scarlett got into a bad marriage to Charles Hamilton, just to spite Ashley, and the addiction ruined her marriage to Rhett."

You know you're addicted to a person when your thoughts are obsessive and the addiction keeps you from living your life,

Tessina explains. One example: You park outside your obsession's apartment all night, and the next day you're too tired to go to work.

Addictions are powerful and difficult to conquer, but they can be overcome. Tessina suggests the following rituals to expunge an addiction from your life.

✦ Banish the person's number from your cell phone. Program the number of a trusted friend, someone you can call when you're itching to call your obsession, in its place.

✦ Set fire to a picture of the two of you together. And don't stop there: "Take everything that reminds you of that person and put it in a far corner of the garage so you don't have to be reminded of it," Tessina says.

✦ Write a letter to your addiction, but don't send it. Burn it. Tessina's a big fan of burning things: "People respond to it—it goes back to really primitive places in our brains."

✦ Visit places that hold memories of your obsession. However, go with a friend "so you can write over those old memories with new ones," Tessina suggests. Old haunts, she adds, are a great place to have an I'm Done with Him/Her ceremony.

✦ Banish the person's name from conversations. If you must use his or her name, think of an alternative, à la He Who Must Not Be Named in the Harry Potter books.

✦ Don't allow your obsession to toy with you. If he or she con-
tinues to call or e-mail, send a simple message: *I don't want
to hear from you.* If the calls persist, use technology to block
that person's telephone number, cell-phone number, and
e-mail.

Scarlett
rule 18

MR. WRONG MAY BE MR. RIGHT

"It's almost like I was in love with him!" she thought, bewildered.
"But I'm not and I just can't understand it."

—Scarlett, *Gone with the Wind*

A man in the house is worth two on the street. —Mae West

He was smart, rich, and handsome. He knew her far better than Ashley, the Tarleton twins, or even her first two husbands. But it took Scarlett a dozen years to realize that of all the men in the South, and probably all the men in the world, Rhett Butler was the one for her.

It wasn't for Rhett's lack of trying. From bidding on her to lead the Virginia reel to buying her that green bonnet in Paris, Rhett made it clear that he was very interested in Scarlett.

Scarlett couldn't help but pick up a few of the hints Rhett dropped. She accepted the bonnet, visited with Rhett when her mother forbade it, and looked forward to those visits with an excitement that made her heart race. Yet, despite so much evidence to the contrary, Scarlett told herself she wasn't in love.

Rhett just wasn't her type. He was a social outcast and many years her senior. He was a man, not a boy happy to tumble at Scarlett's feet, as did her other beaux. Scarlett had no power over Rhett, and for Scarlett, power and love were the same. If she wielded no power over Rhett, her feelings for him could not possibly be love.

When Scarlett finally married Rhett, she was happier than she had ever been in her entire life. Rhett had lots of money, which Scarlett adored, and Rhett was a man in his prime, not a teenager like Charles or prematurely elderly like Frank. But even as she luxuriated in Rhett's wealth and enjoyed their sex life—the first she had had with a grown man who was her physical equal—Scarlett still fought the idea of falling in love with him. For Scarlett, Ashley always came first: in her mind, in her heart, and even, as she lay entwined in Rhett's arms, in her bed.

F*amiliarity breeds contempt. You always want the thing you cannot have. Opposites attract. You don't know what you've got till it's gone.* Dozens of clichés explain why women fall head over heels for Mr. Wrong but can't seem to recognize Mr. Right, even when he shows up at the front door holding a present from Paris.

Mr. Right might be the guy next door, your old high school sweetheart, a childhood friend, or the co-worker in the cube across the way. He's on your side. He supports you even when you've done something wrong. He's your first choice as a companion when you have to attend a wedding or other important event. When you get home from a lousy first date, he's the one you call to tell about it. He gets angry if someone's mistreated you. He's happy when you're happy. You sometimes catch him looking at you in a curious way, but when he notices that you're staring, the look quickly disappears.

You, of course, consider him inconsequential. You take him for granted. You assume he'll always be there to take your late-night calls, listen to your sob stories, and escort you to dinner when everybody else is out of town. And when friends tell you you're great together, that you should date, you dismiss him. "Tom? But we're just friends. We've known each other forever."

Meanwhile, you continue to date Mr. Wrongs, good-looking guys with management jobs, sports cars, beautiful condos, and a knack for choosing the right restaurant. You have—oh, three or four or maybe more dates with each Mr. Wrong, and the relationship always ends badly. He just stops calling. Or you discover his profile is still active on match.com. Or his wife calls you late one night to suggest that you keep away from the father of her children.

But you still steer clear of Mr. Right—until he tells you about *his* great first date or, even more shocking, about his engagement. You're at first astonished (you didn't even know he was dating) and then furious, as furious as Scarlett was when she shoved Rhett's handkerchief, soaked with Belle Watling's perfume, into the woodstove's flames. How could he abandon you? How could he have the nerve to hook up with somebody and leave you stranded in the world of dating?

Be smart. If you have a Mr. Right lurking in the corner cube (and he's not gay, which is sometimes the case with these guys), notice all the hints that Scarlett ignored and turn this guy pal into your boyfriend. The best boyfriend is a woman's fervent cheerleader and avid supporter, her closest confidant, her truest friend. Those great boyfriends make the best husbands, the kind you can trust with your life and your children's lives, the kind you can depend on for better and for worse, the kind you can knock-down-drag-out argue with one moment and roll on the floor laughing with the next.

Scarlett was finally smart enough to marry that "just friends" guy but not smart enough to keep him. Too bad. Were it not for the nagging presence of Ashley, Scarlett and Rhett could have been happy. They were so much alike in their unscrupulousness, their love of material things, and their no-nonsense view of the world.

Looking for love? Scarlett, so much wiser at the end of her tale, undoubtedly would have a suggestion concerning that "just friends" guy you've known forever: *Don't let him get away!*

WHEN MR. RIGHT TURNS INTO MR. WRONG

Rhett left plenty of clues that he had one foot out the door, all of which Scarlett ignored: long absences from home, too much drinking, silence where there had once been taunts and teases. Some relationships with The One don't work out; when it's not working, men drop plenty of hints, says Michael French, author of *Why Men Fall Out of Love: The Secrets They Don't Tell* (Wellness Institute/Self-Help Books, 2005). Here are some.

✦ Physical intimacy wanes. "No matter what excuse he gives, it's something to pay attention to."

✦ His general behavior changes. He's on a new time schedule, he stops seeing old friends, or he acquires a new hobby such as online poker. "He's taking attention away from you and putting it somewhere else."

✦ He starts picking fights. "If things he never even noticed before are a source of irritation, there's something going on."

✦ He stops communicating with you. If he starts making decisions regarding your finances, your household, or your children unilaterally, or leaves them all up to you, "He's disengaging himself," French says.

✦ Out of the blue, he buys you a Cartier bracelet. "Profuse gestures of love and affection can be genuine, but they can be done out of guilt," French says. To find out which, ask what you did to deserve such a great gift. The question "might launch him into confessional mode."

Don't be afraid to discuss these changes with your partner, French suggests. If he's gone and there's a note, you probably can't salvage your relationship. "But as long as you're talking, it's not too late."

Scarlett
rule 19

GIRLFRIENDS MATTER

She had never had a girl friend, and she never felt any lack on that account. —*Gone with the Wind*

Some people go to priests; others to poetry; I to my friends. —Virginia Woolf

Scarlett could have done a lot of things differently: gotten over her crush on Ashley, seen Rhett as her soul mate, chosen not to steal Frank Kennedy from Suellen, been a better mother to her children, or made friends with a few women.

Scarlett found the opposite sex far more useful. Men could be teased and flirted with, relied on in an emergency (that is, if they weren't off fighting a war), and trusted when trust was

called for. Scarlett's best friend was Will Benteen, the poor soldier who stumbled onto Tara's doorstep after the war and
stayed on to give Scarlett a hand. So, when she could, Scarlett
surrounded herself with men.

Excluding women from her life turned out to be one of the
most unfortunate moves that Scarlett ever made. Having no
female friends robbed her of companionship during the war,
when all her beaux and male friends headed off to battle,
most never to return. Having no female friends after the war
forced Scarlett to befriend the despised Republicans, a move
that severed generations-old ties between Scarlett and other
Clayton County families.

If Scarlett chose to have even one female friend, that
friend should have been Melanie. Had Scarlett befriended
Melanie, she would have had as a confidante the bellwether of
Atlanta society. Melanie could have saved Scarlett from em-
barrassment, loss of friends, and more than a little heartache.
But Scarlett chose to go it alone and paid the price.

Perhaps Gloria Steinem was right when she said women
need men like a fish needs a bicycle. But women need
other women as desperately as fish need clean water. Women
who, like Scarlett, think that their husbands and/or boyfriends can take care of all their emotional needs would do
well to think again. All women need at least one trusted female friend, the kind you can ask anything from and, in return, will do anything for.

What do women share with other women that they don't
share with men? Biology, to start with. No man, no matter how

compassionate and in touch with his feminine side, knows what it's like to be pregnant, give birth, or nurse a baby. No man suffers the maddening mood swings of PMS or menopause. When you're going through those life changes, who better to complain to, or to commiserate with, than another woman, even one who hasn't yet had a baby of her own but still can? At least she has the plumbing required to sympathize, if not the experience to empathize. Certain life choices go hand-in-hand with biology. I imagine it would be difficult for a stay-at-home mom to communicate the frustrations and joys of managing a household and raising children to anyone but another stay-at-home mom.

Good salespeople live by the axiom that it's easier to keep existing customers than find new ones, and so it is with friends. Nurture the friendships you have, especially those that stretch back to high school or college. Those women know you. They've seen you through good boyfriends and bad ones, maybe a marriage, perhaps a divorce or two, the births of your children. They know your history; they know what has made you the person you are today. These friends are invaluable. Take care of them, whether they live next door or halfway across the country. Regular e-mails are a fine way to keep each other posted on everyday matters. Phone conversations, even if you must arrange them a month in advance, are better. And there's no substitute for a personal visit. Even if it's once a year, and only for a day, visit your long-distance friends, have them visit you, or meet in a mutually convenient city.

When you make a date with a friend, long-distance or local, keep it, especially if the date's been on your calendars forever. It's respectful of other people's time to keep dates; it's rude to cancel at the last minute and sends a message to your friend that she's not very important to you after all. Try not to cancel a long-standing date with a friend to go out with a guy, unless you want to lose your friend's respect and possibly her friendship.

Take it easy on your girlfriends, especially newer friends whose ties to you are more fragile. If such a friend only seems to call you when she needs a favor—well, if you can help her out, good for you. Isn't it grand to feel helpful? (Besides, you might need that favor returned someday.) If a friend only calls you to complain, listen to her and be grateful that *your* life is a little easier. Try not to indulge in nasty gossip about one friend with another. Gossip wastes precious friendship time and can boomerang in unpleasant ways.

By the same token, try not to be the friend who only calls in time of need. Call or e-mail just to say hello. Drop a card or note in the mail to relieve your gal pals of the mailbox monotony of bills, flyers, and credit-card applications. Send another card or note when you know a friend is going through a tough time.

It's tough to make new friends but not impossible if you decide to take the initiative. No person, man or woman, wants to be the first to extend that invitation for a drink or cup of coffee. So you be the brave one. Consider situations in which you run into the same people regularly: at church, day care, work, or the gym. If you regularly trade light conversation with a woman and you think she's friend material, why not invite her for a cup of coffee or a glass of wine? Of course rejection, which stings no matter which gender it comes from, is entirely possible. Then again, there's a good chance that your potential new friend was thinking of asking you about getting together and will be delighted that you made the first move.

Scarlett didn't have a single female shoulder to cry on when Rhett walked out her door. She'll survive—we know that—but a good friend and a bottle of wine would have made the process a little less painful. If Scarlett had to do it over, she'd make a girlfriend or two and pass along this advice: Men may come and men may go, but girlfriends stick around.

Scarlett lesson

MAKE TIME FOR FRIENDS

Even if Scarlett had friends, making money and trying to spend at least some time with her children would have limited her girlfriend time. Modern women know that the old work–life balance includes kids, jobs, and friends. Here's how some women around the country keep the embers of friendship glowing.

At the beginning of each year I take my calendar and write down all my friends' birthdays on it. I make sure I call or e-mail them, to let them know they are remembered.

—Fran Capo, 37, single with one teenager,
Howard Beach, New York

A couple of times a friend and I go on "walk talks" when we should go to the gym but we really need to talk. We head to a park or walking path and, as we walk, we talk through what we need to. When I'm struggling with a decision, I look forward to the talks—I know my friend will be a good ear.

—Lisa Talamini, 50, married with one teenager,
Carlsbad, California

My friends and I take turns hosting bunko [a dice game] over a themed dinner. The fun comes switching tables every ten minutes or so and getting reconnected with women I may not see on a daily basis. This is the time when I learn what's happening at my kids' schools, engage in a political discussion, and get good tips on clothing, vacations, or a myriad other topics. Hysterical laughter is the order of the evening.

—Denise Davis, 48, married with two teens,
Bakersfield, California

My two college friends and I have birthdays all within a month of one another, so we have devised a yearly weekend getaway called "birthday month." We meet in one of our cities, or in Las Vegas, or at a spa in Palm Springs. It's our one time to get away from the stuff of everyday life. The time just melts away—it's like we are back in college together again.

—Beth McCrae, 42, married, no kids,
Scottsdale, Arizona

Maggie and I have been friends for twenty-two years. We both have families, we own businesses, and so we came up with the idea of going to a day spa quarterly. Every three months we travel an hour through the Columbia Gorge to a spa for a bath, wrap, and massage. Then we split a large seafood salad. We catch up on all the things that are going on and are relaxed "wet noodles" for our husbands. We take a picture every three months to honor the occasion.

—Joanne McCall, 44, married, no kids,

Portland, Oregon

Scarlett
rule 20

BLOOD IS THICKER THAN WATER

They were of her blood, part of Tara. —Gone with the Wind

The other night I ate at a real nice family restaurant. Every table had an argument going. —George Carlin

Had Margaret Mitchell foundered on a name for *Gone with the Wind,* she might well have chosen *Family Ties.* Scarlett's bond to her family and her love for Tara were stronger even than her feelings for Ashley. Scarlett and her family were one and the same; she would not leave them even when leaving would have made her life much easier. Her family and Tara were inextricably entwined; the house embodied Ellen's grace and her rarefied pedigree, while the rolling acres of cotton bespoke Gerald's indomitable immigrant spirit. When Gerald, soothing Scarlett after their argument about Ashley, bid her to admire Tara's sweeping vistas, and later, when Ashley pressed a lump of Tara's cold red clay into her hands, both men were telling Scarlett the same thing: You cannot turn your back on land or family.

No wonder, then, that Scarlett remained loyal to her family even when it was most inconvenient for her to do so. Returning to Tara only to find Ellen dead, Gerald out of his mind with grief, and her sisters weak from typhoid fever, Scarlett's first thought was to split up the family. As quickly as that plan entered her mind, she dismissed it.

Scarlett felt responsible for her family, but she lacked love or even compassion for them, especially her sister Suellen, whom she despised, and her sister Carreen, a fragile soul Scarlett just couldn't love. And neither compassion nor sisterly affection softened Scarlett's grim sense of duty toward Melanie and her son Beau, by far the neediest people at Tara.

But what does it matter if Scarlett cared for her family simply out of loyalty? They were well taken care of all the same. None of them starved or froze to death. Scarlett could have served her family with her mother's selfless compassion; she well might have heeded Ellen's commandment to cherish Suellen and Carreen. But all the love in the world couldn't have fed, clothed, and sheltered those girls as well as Scarlett's hard work did. That end—a safe, comfortable existence—could be said to justify the means.

Sometimes it seems as if family members are meant to detest one another. The saying *You can choose your friends but you can't choose your family* underlines the idea that families are supposed to be tolerated, not loved or cherished. Unemployed brother, annoying sister, alcoholic mom or dad, leering uncle, eccentric aunt—they're all yours to put up with.

It's so much easier to love friends than family; there's much less invested. Friends come without baggage, without history, without nagging memories of who ruined whose Barbie's hairdo; who showed whose boyfriend the naked baby photos on prom night; who got more of Mom's love or less of her nagging. Friends don't have as much invested in us. They don't judge or second-guess as families do; on the other hand, they're far less likely to dole out cash in an emergency or answer the phone at three in the morning.

You love your family most days and on others wish you were an only child and an orphan to boot. The loving days are easy; on the conflicted days, follow Rule 9 and just do it. Fighting the flow of family life is far more difficult, time-consuming, and vexing than simply floating along with it. Consider, for example, the passive-aggressive script followed by thousands, if not millions, of Americans every holiday season.

YOU: Mom, I'm not coming for Christmas dinner.

MOM: What? Why not? I ordered a honey-baked ham just for you. And your uncle Bobby will be there. You love your uncle Bobby!

YOU: Sorry, I made other plans. I'm going to Sarah's house this year.

MOM: Sarah's! What will her family think, that you spend a holiday with strangers!

YOU: I don't care what they think. They invited me and I'm going and that's that.

MOM: (*Changing her tone*) Oh, please, honey . . .

Such conversations rarely end in resolution. They are frustrating, stressful, and not festive at all. Here's an alternative.

YOU: Hi, Mom. What time is dinner on Sunday?

MOM: Seven. Could you bring dessert?

YOU: Sure, no problem! See you then. Love you! Bye!

Assuming that your childhood was only garden-variety unhappy (the only kind worth living, according to memoirist Frank McCourt) and that you did not experience a trauma that's landed you in therapy (plenty of such traumas exist), isn't it easier and far less stressful to have the second conversation than the first?

It's easier, but it takes some work to get there. The trick is to step out of the role (meek sister, argumentative mother, defiant daughter) you've been playing your whole life.

Does your brother dangle some ancient bait that he knows you'll rise to? Refuse to take it. Does your mother continue to load your plate long after you're full? "Thanks, Mom, I'm full." This is not easy, but with diligent practice beforehand it can be done. If it's just too difficult, or if you need to rehearse your new role a few more times, try an abbreviated dinner.

Make a polite exit after the entrée or show up for dessert, a bottle of champagne in hand.

Between family dinners, it's helpful to touch base with family members every so often. The inventors of e-mail will probably never know how many families they've saved. And birthday cards: The circumstance of your birth is the very thing that makes you family, so isn't it a good idea to acknowledge family birthdays? If the sentiments of fake, overwritten mass-made greeting cards turn your stomach, buy cards meant for little kids. They're bright, amusing, and cheaper than grown-up varieties and, best of all, they rhyme.

Between family dinners, try not to take sides, one set of siblings against another. A corollary to this piece of advice: Accept your family members for who they are, what they do, and the decisions they make. The linguist Deborah Tannen makes a grand point in her book *I Only Say This Because I Love You* (Random House, 2001): Family members say many destructive things in the name of love. When Tannen's phrase bubbles on your lips, rethink what you're about to say and perhaps keep it to yourself. Trust your adult family members to live their lives *their* way, and chances are they'll let you live your life *your* way.

Scarlett knew that loyalty transcends love; she didn't have to love or even like her family to feel and act on her deep sense of responsibility toward them. Love without loyalty would have been worthless; her loyalty, even without love, saved their lives. *There's* something to talk about at the next family dinner.

Scarlett lesson

MANAGING THE SISTER ACT

Scarlett committed the mother of all sister sins when she stole Frank Kennedy from Suellen. "It's the ultimate rivalry . . . it creates a rift that might never be healed," says Susan Shapiro Barash, a sociologist and author of *Sisters: Devoted or Divided* (Replica Books, 2001). Even without such thievery, the sister act can be difficult, especially for sisters with a bit of rivalry or jealousy in their past. Barash offers a few suggestions on how to stay on good terms with your sister; not surprisingly, her advice works for brothers, too.

✦ Just because you're sisters doesn't mean you're automatically close. "That's one of the great myths," Barash says.

✦ Be generous of spirit, even if your sister isn't. "Your relationship today and tomorrow matters more than the past."

✦ Get rid of old patterns. Acknowledge topics that irritate each other (perhaps wildly opposing views on politics or child rearing) and agree to avoid those subjects in each other's company.

✦ Recognize that you are different people with different perspectives. "What you interpret as terrific about your mother, your sister might see as destructive," Barash explains. Try to respect your sister's interpretation of your childhood, as off-base as it might sound.

✦ Try not to be overly critical of your sister. "Appreciate what she offers that's unique."

✦ When all else fails, try food. "Make an effort to bring family, spouses, and children together for a family dinner—it's the gesture that counts."

And do try to maintain ties with your sister, not only for emotional reasons but for practical ones, Barash says. One day you might need to team with her to care for elderly parents or handle another difficult family situation.

Scarlett
rule 21

Oh, the jealous fools who said money wasn't everything!

—Scarlett, *Gone with the Wind*

The only way not to think about money is to have a great deal of it.

—Edith Wharton

Whirling around the dance floor with Rhett in the early days of the war, Scarlett felt financially secure enough to toss off a comment: "Money can't buy everything." Ever the cynic, Rhett scornfully disagreed. Scarlett floundered for a retort, because as far as she knew, Rhett was right. In her seventeen years, Scarlett had wanted for nothing. Gerald's money bought her all she needed, and then some. Even as Clayton County boys headed to battle in droves and the econ-

omy built on King Cotton began to crumble, Scarlett didn't
think about money. She didn't have to.

Four years later, Scarlett had absolutely nothing to worry
about *but* money and where to find some, because she had
none. Once owner of a vast wardrobe, she was down to a single
ragged dress. The Confederate money that Gerald had stock-
piled was worthless; the substantial wealth Scarlett stood to
inherit was reduced to the greenbacks and twenty dollars in
gold she found in the wallet of the Yankee soldier she had
murdered.

The dead Yankee's money was Scarlett's seed money, the
start-up capital that enabled her to turn Tara into a thriving
farm. Unlike the dot-coms in the go-go nineties that burned
through venture capital at a dizzying rate, Scarlett took good
care of that Yankee money—and the money she made after
that, too.

Even after the threat of starvation had long passed, Scarlett stayed smart about money. Once Scarlett had her hands on
Frank's store, mill, and savings, she spun them into gold. She
used the profits from one mill to buy another. She persuaded
Frank's deadbeat customers to pay the debts Frank had all but
forgiven. And it's worth saying again that she did this at a time
when, if women were allowed to make money at all, it was
only a modest amount and then only via such feminine occupations as baking, sewing, and painting china.

Hard work, not luck, got Scarlett her money, but she was
lucky in one respect. When she married Rhett, she married a
man who allowed her to keep her own earnings. By law, Rhett
could easily have commandeered every dime of Scarlett's for
his own use. But Rhett, who was proud of his wife's business

sense, not to mention far richer than she was, let Scarlett keep what she had. Sometimes their cash pots mingled (to build Scarlett's garish dream house, for example), but when it came to supporting the mill that Ashley managed, Scarlett was on her own. A double-income couple discussing whose money to spend on what: how contemporary. Scarlett and Rhett could have been two Wall Street bankers lounging at their club.

Were Scarlett a Wall Street banker and not a plantation owner's daughter, she would be perched in a luxurious penthouse overlooking Central Park. Scarlett loved the finer things in life. And she knew, better than anyone else, what hard work it takes to pay for them.

Money makes the world go round; there is no better evidence of that than reality TV. If not for money, why on earth would people eat weird things, live on a deserted island with strangers, date twenty men (or women) at the same time, or jump through hoops to land a job with a New York real-estate developer? Americans, however, tend to be perennially short of cash. The average American household's credit-card debt today is $8,400. The average household pays $1,200 a year in credit-card interest. Forty percent of American families spend more than they earn.

To avoid that fate—or spring free from it—consider the following maxims, translated to apply to the world of personal finance. Scarlett, practically a nineteenth-century Suze Orman, would approve.

A penny saved is a penny earned

Scarlett saved every penny possible; if she'd had the choice, she would have invested that money under the floorboard in a 401(k). She knew that by saving she was investing in her future.

Chance favors the prepared

Scarlett's savings, plus a good relationship with Rhett and his millions, allowed her to buy a second mill at a bargain-basement price, thus adding to her business empire.

The harder you work, the luckier you get

Curiously, although she was brought up to do nothing more difficult than flirt, Scarlett knew the value of hard work. She worked from sunup to sundown at Tara and spent full days at her store and her mill.

Waste not, want not

Scarlett rued Tara's waste of food before the war; at each meal the table groaned with platters of enough food to feed the Confederate Army. Afterward, she (and the entire South) recycled clothes until they were rags, lined shoes with cardboard, and in the morning drank "coffee" made from parched corn and ground yams.

Haste makes waste

Think before you shop; panic-buying a brand-new outfit two hours before a big event is rarely a good idea. Unless you are an ace shopper, like Carrie on *Sex and the City*, you will pay too much for your new outfit, wear it once, and then never again.

A stitch in time saves nine

Well-tended possessions look better and last longer than mistreated items. So repair that inch of unraveling hem before the whole thing comes down. Hang up your clothes after work, wash your car regularly, and take care of minor home repairs before they blossom into expensive projects.

Once bitten, twice shy

Feel free to learn from your past financial errors. If your friends persuaded you to buy a three-thousand-dollar Marc Jacobs jacket and you nearly passed out when you got your Visa bill—well, wear the jacket in good health. But don't let friends pressure you into overspending again. If you're easily tempted, shop alone.

There's no free lunch

All freebies—trial subscriptions for magazines, a vacation where you listen to a time-share pitch, even a two-for-one coupon at your favorite restaurant—cost you time at the very least and usually money. Scarlett learned the no-free-lunch rule from Rhett: He loaned her money to buy another mill, but on condition that the mill not support Ashley.

Clueless in some areas of life, Scarlett was razor-sharp when it came to money. Save your pennies, she'd tell a woman focused more on shopping than saving. You'll need them someday.

MONEY MOVES YOU CAN'T NOT MAKE

Scarlett was good at making money, keeping it, and investing what she made. Sharon Durling, a former bond broker and author of *A Girl and Her Money* (W Publishing Group, 2003), works with women who aren't as money-smart as Scarlett, and for them she offers the smartest money moves any woman can make.

✦ Spend less than you earn, save the difference, and invest in something you understand. "Don't go with Cousin Vinnie's hot tip; don't buy a complicated investment some broker is hawking."

✦ Know where your money goes. For three solid months, track every single expenditure, from your rent to your daily latte. The results will indicate your financial priorities, which you can adjust if they don't match your real priorities. For example: You might not consider yourself a clothes-horse until you discover that 75 percent of your disposable income ends up at Nordstrom.

✦ Read your credit-card statements. You should keep track of what you're billed for; believe it or not, Durling says, sometimes credit-card companies make mistakes.

✦ Don't nickel-and-dime yourself to financial ruin. Eating lunch out every day, even if it's only a seven-dollar sand-wich, or making weekly garage sale purchases ("It was only five bucks!") add up faster than you think.

✦ Keep your eye on your own financial ball. What your friends wear or drive, where they go on vacation, and what kind of houses they live in—this has nothing to do with you; spending money is not a competition. "Don't let some-one else's values run your life," Durling says.

Scarlett
rule 22

BUT MONEY ISN'T EVERYTHING

"Damn our money! All our money can't buy what I want for her."
—Rhett to Scarlett, *Gone with the Wind*

For thy sweet love remember'd such wealth brings
That then I scorn to change my state with kings'.
—William Shakespeare, Sonnet 29

Scarlett worked hard for her money. She devoted all her strength and all her brainpower to stockpiling as much financial security as she could. How sad to learn that her security stretched only so far and her safety didn't extend beyond the food in her pantry, the clothes in her closet, and the roof over her head. Scarlett knew money could buy the food, clothes, and luxuries she so missed when she was poor. But the knowledge that money cannot buy intangibles—love, happiness, a sense of well-being—eluded her.

Scarlett could hardly be blamed for equating wealth with happiness. The daughter of a wealthy planter, she had had as much food as she wanted, beautiful dresses to spare, and an active social life. Wrapped in all that comfort, Scarlett never understood that her health, her pleasing (at least when she wanted it to be) personality, and her parents' love for her contributed as much to her general state of happiness as did her father's money.

As Scarlett grew rich after the war, and as her memories of hunger faded, there were signs that she wasn't happy. Her recurring nightmare was not the dream of a contented person. She pined for Ashley well after a happy woman would have abandoned such a girlish longing. She confessed to Rhett that amid her riches she was lonely; happy people are not lonely.

As ignorantly as Scarlett equated wealth with happiness, she also equated wealth with gentility. She believed that Ellen was a generous, kind gentlewoman only because Ellen had the time and finances to be generous, kind, and gentle. Myopic as she was, Scarlett couldn't see that after the war, Melanie, living in her small, shabby house, remained the standard-bearer for old Southern chivalry and grace.

Finally, Scarlett mistakenly believed that when she was rich nothing bad would ever happen to her again. She could not have been more wrong. Her money didn't prevent Gerald from tumbling off his horse and breaking his neck; Rhett's money couldn't keep their darling daughter Bonnie from meeting the same fate. And the heavy, expensive carved door on Scarlett's house couldn't hold Rhett locked inside; when he wanted to leave, he sailed through that door, free as a bird. When Rhett said to Scarlett, "My dear, I don't give a damn," he could easily have been talking about her money.

L ife is easier with money than without money. As wags are fond of pointing out, it's more fun to be unhappy *with* money than unhappy *without* it; you can always bundle up your unhappiness and take it to the South of France for a little getaway.

Still, as Scarlett discovered perhaps too late, money does not have unlimited power. It can soothe unhappiness but not dispel it. It can buy grand houses but not fill those houses with healthy, happy, long-lived people. A big-enough bank account can lure a woman into marriage but can hardly guarantee a contented, fulfilling relationship. Money can buy tuition at a good college but not an education; education takes discipline and hard work.

Real-life examples abound; there's an embarrassment of riches, you might even say. If money could buy a happy marriage, Brad and Jen would still be together; for that matter, Angelina and Billy Bob would still be wearing vials of each other's blood around their necks. If money could buy a happy life, Woolworth heiress Barbara Hutton (for three years Mrs. Cary Grant) would not have ended up a sad alcoholic.

While Scarlett focused on money as life's biggest treasure, she was rich in ways that extended beyond her fat bank balance. Here are some of the other treasures she enjoyed.

Her health
Scarlett—until she fell down the stairs and suffered a miscarriage—wasn't sick a day in her life. She recovered from her children's births quickly and enjoyed an abundance of energy, too.

The ability to have fun
Some people are rich and don't enjoy their money; not Scarlett. Sure, she pinched pennies at the beginning, but when she finally felt rich enough, she built an outlandish house, decorated it with the best furnishings money could buy, and entertained lavishly.

Two true friends
Melanie didn't care whether Scarlett was the belle of Tara, the owner of a run-down plantation, or Atlanta's richest woman; she stuck by her friend whatever their circumstances. Scarlett would have been so much happier had she enjoyed Melanie's friendship rather than fought it. And Will Benteen, the poor soldier who convalesced at Tara, did whatever needed to be done—and even did Scarlett the grand favor of marrying Suellen.

Money to spare
Scarlett had just as much fun writing checks to her mother's sisters and sending Will Benteen money for Tara's upkeep as she did planning her fancy parties. As selfish as she could be, even Scarlett realized the benefit of giving money away.

Scarlett let herself think that enough money could fend off all of life's travails. True, money helped solve some of her problems, but for others, Scarlett's money wasn't worth the paper it was printed on.

Scarlett
lesson

MORE THAN MONEY

Scarlett lavished attention on her finances yet ignored nearly every other aspect of her life. Women who'd prefer to be happier than Scarlett should invest time and care in their entire lives, says Pamela York Klainer, a financial consultant and author of *How Much Is Enough?: Harness the Power of Your Money Story—and Change Your Life* (Basic Books, 2001). "Let money do what money does and look elsewhere for other things," Klainer says. In her view, here are the ingredients for a well-lived life.

✦ *Intimate relationships.* "We need other people for support, love, and fun," Klainer says. Make friends and socialize with them.

✦ *Comfort in your chosen role.* Whether it's as a full-time mother, full-time wife, caregiver, career woman, or social butterfly, find satisfaction in it.

✦ *A sense of competence.* Do your absolute best at work; if you're a full-time mom, test your capabilities in what

Klainer calls a "neutral arena." "We have to test ourselves in places where nobody has a vested interest in telling us how wonderful we are."

♦ *Acceptance of the consequences of your decisions.* Mature, well-considered moves—for example, the decision to leave a relationship—often hurt other people. That can't be helped. "It's part of life," Klainer says.

♦ *Full involvement in life.* Join a political campaign or the neighborhood cleanup crusade, or find some other way to "get yourself out there and try to make something happen," Klainer urges.

Scarlett
rule 23

"What I've wished for so often has happened."

—Scarlett, *Gone with the Wind*

Life is what happens when you're busy making other plans.

—John Lennon

Scarlett was a planner, a strategic thinker, a woman who looked into the future and tried to plan for its every twist and turn. Her ability to envision her future as she wanted, no *if*s or *but*s intruding, was probably the main reason she reached so many of her goals.

Even after the war, when life was so uncertain that a person couldn't bank on being alive one day to the next, much less plan for the future, Scarlett kept on plotting and planning. She and her crew at Tara planted cotton, harvested it, and baled it; that cotton, she decided, would help build her future.

And as she planned and plotted, Scarlett worried. She worried what the family would eat for its next meal and where, exactly, that food would come from. She worried, always, that the Union Army or a single malicious soldier would show up once again to loot Tara or worse. She worried that her son, Wade, wasn't maturing properly. On one of the few occasions when Scarlett let her mind rest, when she dared be satisfied with the present, her reward was a most unpleasant surprise: Her carefully hoarded cotton went up in smoke.

Such hard lessons taught Scarlett that the future was a safer place than the present—and a far safer place than the past. The single time Scarlett allowed herself a reminiscence, sitting in her mill's office with Ashley on the day of his surprise birthday party, her punishment was swift and tough: Caught up in their memories of dances and parties, twilight horseback rides, and the scent of Tara's magnolia blossoms, Ashley embraced Scarlett just as Mrs. Meade and India walked through the mill's front door. To them, that innocent embrace was as damning as if Scarlett and Ashley had been caught naked and writhing on the floor.

Because Scarlett was so involved in the future, she rarely invested the slightest emotional energy in the present, and that lack of investment was one of her sharpest failures. Busy orchestrating tomorrow, she relegated care of her children to Melanie. And though Scarlett was smart, she didn't concern herself with current affairs. As a result, many events caught her by surprise: the war itself, that the Confederacy lost, and that the new government wanted more tax money from her.

Scarlett thought all her planning would insulate her from future shocks. She never figured out, as wise people do, that tomorrow and today are intertwined; even though tomorrow is an abstraction, what happens in the present has some bearing on the future. And she didn't take advantage of present opportunities. When Rhett left her, she didn't decide to relax and perhaps become reacquainted with her children. No; she immediately began plotting to win Rhett back.

Caught up in her future, Scarlett never did figure out that "life is what happens when you're busy making other plans."

Thanks to the technological advances of the Information Age, it's easier than ever to lose focus on the here and now. It's possible to read a newspaper online, check e-mail, get the weather forecast, catch up with a friend, plug a doctor's appointment into a PDA, and drive to the store, pretty much all at the same time. The results are sometimes comical: people walking around with tiny phones clamped to their ears. What once would be fodder for a *Saturday Night Live* sketch passes for normal.

Technology is fun, and it does feel contemporary to have so many high-tech toys and do so many things at once. But it can be overwhelming. Don't you sometimes feel at the end of a day that, despite all you have accomplished, you can't remember a single isolated event or project? That you have to sit down and concentrate to remember what you had for lunch, and with whom, or whether you managed to read the day's paper? Living here, there, and everywhere but the moment can sap satisfaction as easily as it can make work time ten times more productive.

Just for one day, try trading productivity for satisfaction. Try to enjoy each of life's minutes as they arrive. Try to slow down, to accomplish one task at a time and do it well. Your family and colleagues might think you're crazy, but chances are good that you'll end the day feeling relaxed and happy. Here's a to-do list for a live-in-the-moment day; pick and choose at will or come up with ideas of your own.

Don't schedule anything

If that's not possible for an entire day, try for a morning or afternoon. Let the unscheduled time be yours to unfold as it might. Let yourself be bored. Let your mind wander. Take a nap. Do what you are moved to do.

Focus on one task at a time

Talk on the phone *or* check e-mail, not both simultaneously. Drive *or* have a cell-phone conversation, not both. Make a choice: TV *or* a phone conversation. *Note:* This does not apply to time-intensive tasks, such as laundry, unless you think you'd enjoy hours of watching your clothes swirl in the washer and tumble in the dryer.

Eat breakfast, lunch, and dinner alone

Not without human companionship, but without reading or watching TV. Savor the three meals of your live-in-the-moment day. Enjoy the food and enjoy the presence of your dining companion.

Wait in a long line

Observe what's going on around you; investigate your neighbor's cart. Eavesdrop. If it's a familiar store, look for five or ten things you've never noticed before.

Leave your personal stereo at home

Walk or run and absorb the sounds of your neighborhood—the birds, the squeal of tires, the sound of a car starting, the drone of a TV from inside a house, a baby crying, kids laughing on the playground. Even go-go Scarlett occasionally took time to enjoy the beauty of Tara.

Don't wear a watch

Do you really need to check the time every ten minutes? Probably not. It's so nice to wander, especially on a Saturday or a holiday, without the construct of time hanging over your head. If you need to know the hour, find a clock or ask somebody.

Let yourself flow

Why quit an absorbing task—reading, walking, rearranging a room—just because the big hand on the clock points to a certain number? Those who have been there know there's no place like *flow:* the ineffable feeling of being so completely and utterly consumed by a job that time loses all meaning.

Contemporary women are too much like Scarlett in this respect: We're so busy *doing* that we don't take time to just *be.* Learn from Scarlett's mistake and slow down.

BE A DAYDREAM BELIEVER

Nothing stops time like a daydream: a moment when your mind exits reality, a moment when anything is possible. While she probably didn't realize it, Scarlett was a great daydreamer, allowing herself little reveries in which hunger and poverty didn't exist. "Scarlett acted on her daydreams, and she let herself have her daydreams," says F. Diane Barth, a Manhattan clinical social worker and author of *Daydreaming: Unlock the Creative Power of Your Mind* (Penguin, 1997). Daydreaming, Barth says, provides a fantastic if only momentary escape from reality—and it can help solve problems, too. Try it.

✦ Make space for daydreams. Staring off into space might appear unproductive, "but when you daydream you are very busy," Barth says.

✦ Daydream whenever you want. You don't need to be curled up in a chair, gazing out a window. Barth daydreams when she does laundry.

✦ Let your mind wander. Don't program your daydream. "The fun of it is to see where your mind goes."

✦ Take daydreams figuratively, not literally. A daydream of a carefree month in France might never come true, but it could lead you to plan a long-overdue vacation.

✦ Pay attention to recurring daydreams. Just like a recurring night dream, a persistent daydream might be a sign that some aspect of your life needs attention.

✦ Keep a daydream notebook. "Writing them down gives you a chance to let daydreams live," Barth says, "and that's the most important thing."

Scarlett rule 24

TOMORROW IS ANOTHER DAY

"Tomorrow, I'll think of some way to get him back."

—Scarlett, *Gone with the Wind*

Never put off until tomorrow what you can do the day after tomorrow.

—Mark Twain

So much happened to Scarlett—from the day she perched on Tara's front steps, flirting with the Tarleton twins, to the day she sat dejectedly on her red-carpeted staircase, watching Rhett leave, perhaps forever. She married three times and buried two husbands; she bore three children and lost one. She committed murder. She lied, stole, and cheated. She gained love and lost it. Through it all, she didn't do what many women would be sorely tempted to do: get drunk, retreat under the covers, jump off a high bridge. Not Scarlett. When life became too much for her to handle, and it often did, Scarlett trotted out the philosophy that has become as iconic as that green velvet dress.

As handily as her just-do-it attitude and as crucially as her velvet-curtain resourcefulness, Scarlett's ability to invoke tomorrow helped her survive ordeals that very likely would break an ordinary woman. Oh, yes, occasionally Scarlett invoked *tomorrow* for the same reason an ostrich sticks its head in the sand: to avoid unpleasant truths.

Far more usefully, Scarlett summoned *tomorrow* as a temporary escape from life. When she was too tired to take another step, to think another thought, to make a productive move, Scarlett called for *tomorrow* and called it quits. She knew herself well enough to know when to say when. When the responsibility of caring for Tara and her family grew overwhelming, Scarlett said *enough*. When she was near tears, thinking about her dead mother or feeble father, Scarlett said *enough*. And when she came even close to considering that Ashley might never return from the war, she quickly stuffed that notion into her *tomorrow* file.

But *tomorrow* didn't always work. Lying in the Twelve Oaks garden with the house's ruins in plain view, just after her aching stomach heaved up a radish, Scarlett tried but failed to push away thoughts of the war's death and devastation. By the end of her story, her *tomorrow* charm completely lost its potency. Melanie died just when Scarlett discovered how much she loved and needed her. Ashley was hers when she no longer wanted him, and all the tomorrows in the world would change neither fact. Yet hours later Scarlett was back to her old self, summoning *tomorrow* to give herself time to lure Rhett back to their marriage and back in love with her.

On the one hand, Scarlett used *tomorrow* as an excuse for ethically dicey behavior: Marrying Frank, offering to be Rhett's mistress, lusting for Ashley, and leasing the convicts were among her favorite *tomorrow* topics. On the other hand, *tomorrow* let Scarlett concentrate on her formidable challenges: surviving after the war, scratching an existence out of almost nothing for herself and nine other people, and living with adversity when she was accustomed to living in comfort.

Tomorrow let Scarlett be Scarlett: a warts-and-all survivor and one of the most fascinating and believable characters in American literature.

Tomorrow is a tricky business. How do you decide when to postpone a decision or a thought and when it's time to soldier on? When does *tomorrow* save time and sanity, and at what point does it become old-fashioned procrastination? When will you applaud your wise decision to invoke *tomorrow*, and when will you regret it forever?

Some actions and decisions simply can't wait until morning. *Tomorrow* won't do when a contract or offer is ready to expire. (How many hesitant buyers have lost their dream house because they stalled?) A need-it-now work project with a complicated time line involving several departments shouldn't wait until the next day, if for no other reason than to give you the right to say "don't blame me" (but you wouldn't) when the project runs into overtime. On April 15, *tomorrow* is not a good idea.

Many health matters can't wait. That lump, unexplained stomachache, or persistent headache? Get it looked at today, not tomorrow, even if it means an expensive and unpleasant trip to the emergency room. A sickening *crack* when you fall off your bike and hit the pavement? Today, gentle reader, not tomorrow.

Certain love matters can't wait. On February 14, *tomorrow* is a bad idea indeed, especially if your partner is the romantic sort who sets great store by flowers, candlelit dinners, and big boxes of chocolates. *Today* is also infinitely better when it comes to anniversaries and birthdays; such occasions can lose sparkle when they're celebrated early or late. Sometimes relationships can't wait until tomorrow. If he wants to take things to the next level and makes a reasonable offer, a mature person can't cry *tomorrow* for very long. Certain discussions can't wait, including ones involving lipstick on a collar or a suspicious note found in a pants pocket; such discoveries should spark a right-here, right-now conversation, not a slow smoldering of anger and mistrust. And whoever dreamed up the marriage rule *Never go to bed angry* knew what she was talking about.

Tomorrow or today might depend on your personality. Some types save nothing for morning. They're up past midnight paying bills, doing dishes, grooming dogs, and answering e-mails until every last item on their to-do list has a check mark next to it. Other types delay chores, bills, and e-mails until the last second and then tackle them all in one frantic swoop. Or they wait until a deadline is too close to ignore; some feel the muse sitting on their shoulder only under intense pressure.

Scarlett used the present to do what she had to; she used the future as a filing cabinet for less tangible projects. She rarely opened that filing cabinet to retrieve those projects; most gathered dust as Scarlett went about the business of becoming rich. The very last project Scarlett filed was convincing Rhett, just as he had convinced her, that they were soul mates and belonged together. When Scarlett lifted her chin, summoned her sky-high self-esteem, and conjured up Tara, her port in any storm, faithful readers knew that Scarlett would indeed get Rhett back. Today? Perhaps not. But tomorrow? Definitely.

EFFECTIVE PROCRASTINATION

Never put off till tomorrow what you can do today. That's what well-meaning mothers counsel, but Scarlett thought differently: *Always put off whatever you can till tomorrow.* Scarlett was a fan of putting off thinking until morning, but plenty of tasks can wait till morning as well. Here are a few.

Dishes or housework. The dishes won't sneak out the back door in the middle of the night; unless you have a very special dog, she won't vacuum the living room while you're asleep.

Financial work. Leave it until morning, especially if you're tired or jet-lagged. A weary mind makes mistakes.

A major decision. Spinning your wheels? Sleep on it. Who knows, a dream might provide a solution.

An argument. Go to bed and cuddle instead. You can revisit your disagreement in the morning.

A criticism. Plan your verbal attack but wait twenty-four hours before launching it. At the very least, walk the dog first.

Watching TV. Invest in TiVo or simply let yourself miss an episode of *Desperate Housewives*. It's not tough to catch up.

Whatever you're about to do when a better offer comes along. Step away from the ironing board. Put down that paring knife. Get dressed, grab your bag, and dash out the door. Save the housework—for tomorrow.

AFTERWORD

I have several hopes for *Scarlett Rules* and its readers.

I hope that skeptics can suspend disbelief and embrace Scarlett O'Hara, a fictional character, as a role model as legitimate as any flesh-and-blood woman. The concept is not unusual; Carrie, Charlotte, Miranda, and Samantha of *Sex and the City* have inspired legions of young women to be more assertive in relationships, worry less about being single, and, let's not forget, wear Manolos. Jerry Seinfeld and his sidekicks, Elaine, George, and Kramer, inspired legions to look at humor in an entirely different way.

I hope readers accept Scarlett, despite her hoopskirts and whalebone stays, as a relevant model for those of us living in the twenty-first century. I hope readers find Scarlett, as I do, a timeless character faced with timeless choices.

I hope that, after finishing *Scarlett Rules*, readers embrace their own imperfections. Scarlett is fascinating because she is so brazenly imperfect; for every right move she makes, she makes at least two wrong ones. To err is not only human, it's delightful, and in the pages of *Gone with the Wind* it's one reason why Scarlett is so much more compelling than Melanie. Most of all, I hope that *Scarlett Rules* encourages readers who've only visited *Gone with the Wind* once—as well as those who've only seen the movie—to reread the novel and discover some of their own Scarlett Rules.

The twenty-four rules presented on these pages are based on major events in Scarlett's life: her crush on Ashley, the Civil War, her struggle to rise out of poverty, her complicated friendship and even more complicated romance with Rhett Butler. However, they're filtered through my own experiences. I brought my life in its various stages—awkward teen, searching young adult, reasonably self-confident woman—to each reading of *Gone with the Wind* and drew a different lesson from it each time. In the same way, each reader will bring her or his own life to the pages and, I hope, find different, perhaps more personal, guidelines.

If it is not to be *Gone with the Wind,* I hope my adventures with Scarlett will prompt readers to revisit their own favorite novel, one featuring a strong, realistic character rich with strengths and even richer with faults. Role models exist in real life but they also exist in literature, even more deliciously because all we have of them is what's between the covers of the book. No gossip column can sully a fictional hero's reputation; no celebrity magazine can come between a girl and her fictional heroine. I've learned so much, not only from Scarlett O'Hara but from Jo March, Lily Bart, and even Bridget Jones. I wish my readers the same literary good fortune.

ACKNOWLEDGMENTS

Thanks to Margaret Mitchell for creating the immortal Scarlett.

Thanks to Leslie Levine for introducing me to Nicole Diamond Austin, whose faith in this project and in me are key to its existence. I thank Debra Goldstein for taking over where Nicole left off.

Thanks to my editor, Christina Duffy, for her enthusiasm, vision, and insightful edits.

Thank you to Carolyn Bertagnoli, Laurie Bertagnoli, and Jim Bertagnoli, who inspire me more than they know.

Thanks to James L. Swanson, author and Lincoln scholar, for firmly suggesting that I put my love of Scarlett to good use, and to photographer Kingmond Young for his generous gifts of time and talent.

And most of all, thanks to William Schober, my Rhett Butler, Ashley Wilkes, and Will Benteen all rolled up into one fine package. I don't know what I'd do without you.

Lisa Bertagnoli writes about style, culture, restaurants, business, and the arts for a variety of newspapers
and magazines. She lives in Chicago.